Piano • Vocal • Guitar

LOVE SONGS from
BROADWAY

1980s to Today

ISBN 978-1-4234-5390-1

HAL • LEONARD®
CORPORATION

7777 W. BLUEMOUND RD. P.O. BOX 13819 MILWAUKEE, WI 53213

Visit Hal Leonard Online at
www.halleonard.com

ALL I ASK OF YOU
from THE PHANTOM OF THE OPERA

Music by ANDREW LLOYD WEBBER
Lyrics by CHARLES HART
Additional Lyrics by RICHARD STILGOE

RAOUL: No more talk of dark-ness, for-get these wide-eyed fears: I'm

here, noth-ing can harm you, my words will warm and calm you.

Let me be your free-dom, let day-light dry your tears: I'm

AS LONG AS YOU'RE MINE

from the Broadway Musical WICKED

Music and Lyrics by
STEPHEN SCHWARTZ

With quiet passion

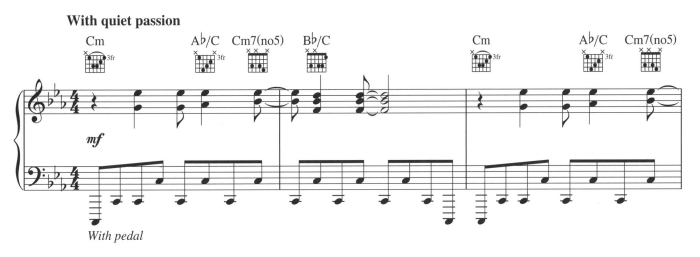

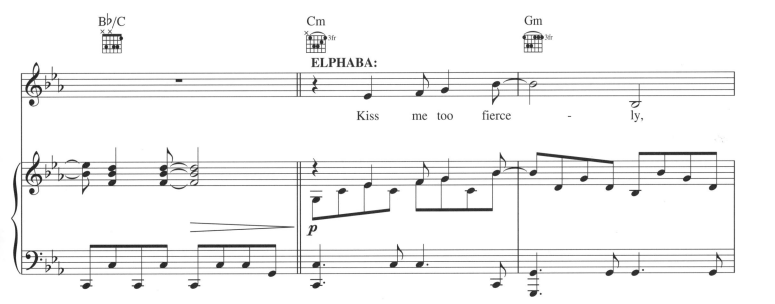

ELPHABA:

Kiss me too fierce - ly,

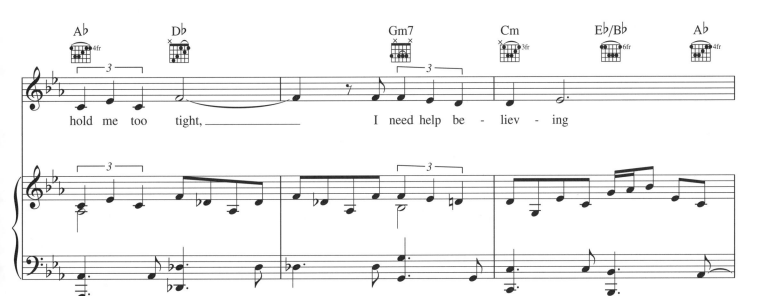

hold me too tight, _____ I need help be - liev - ing

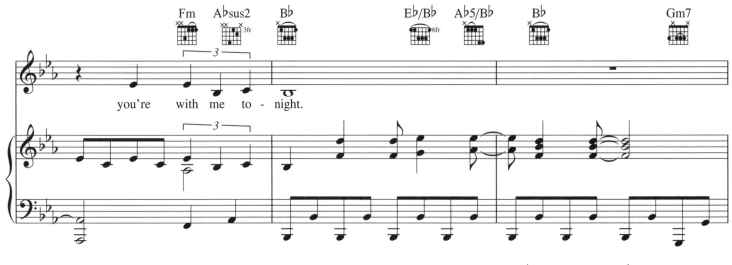

you're with me to - night.

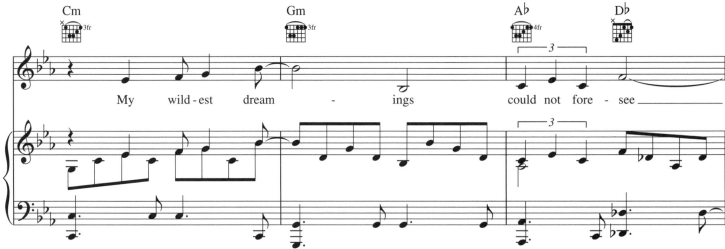

My wild - est dream - ings could not fore - see ___

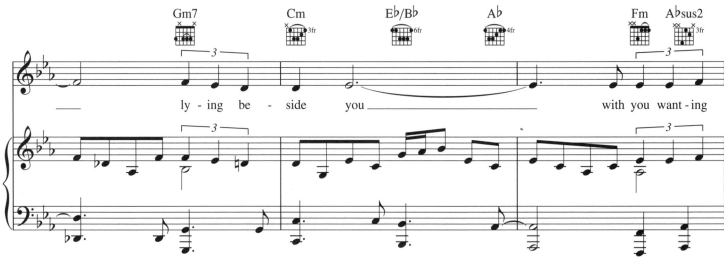

___ ly - ing be - side you ___ with you want - ing

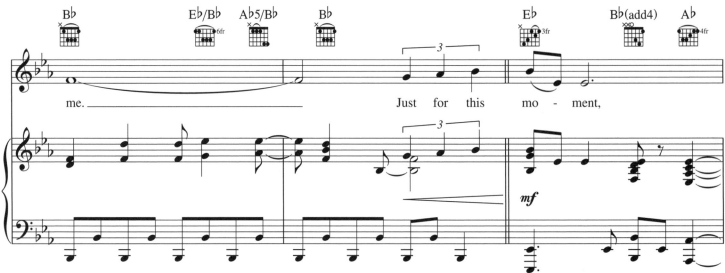

me. ___ Just for this mo - ment,

as long as you're mine, I've lost all re-

sist - ance _____ and crossed some bor - der - line. __

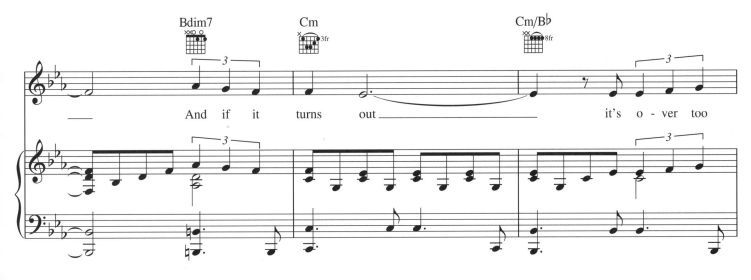

And if it turns out _____ it's o - ver too

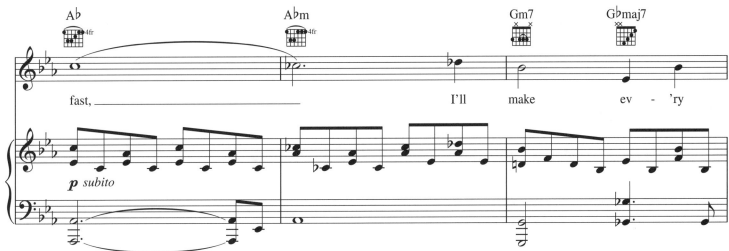

fast, _____ I'll make ev - 'ry

p subito

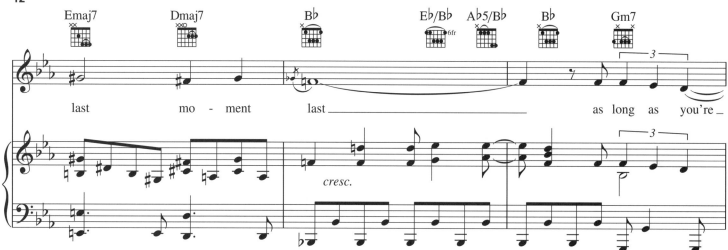

last mo-ment last _____ as long as you're ___

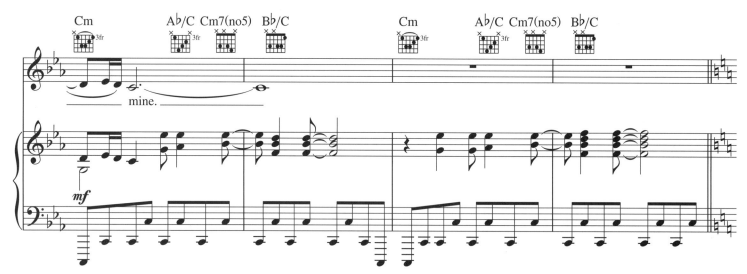

___ mine.

FIYERO:

May-be I'm brain - less, may-be I'm wise, _____

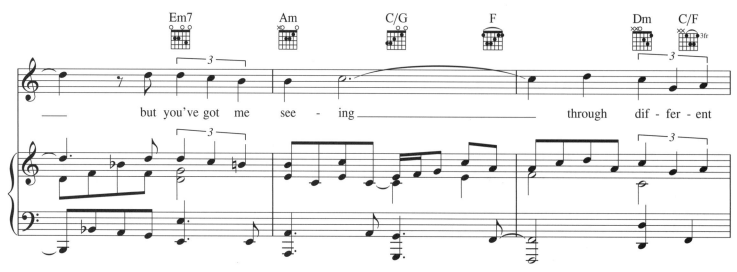

___ but you've got me see - ing _____ through dif-fer-ent

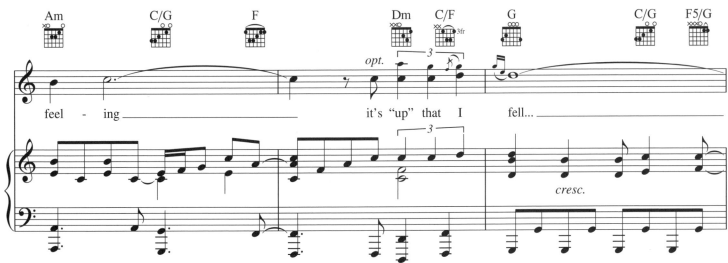

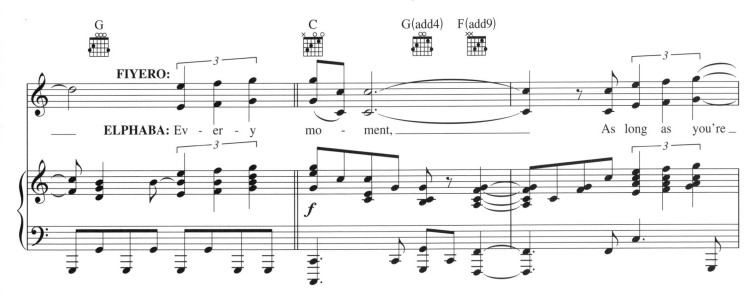

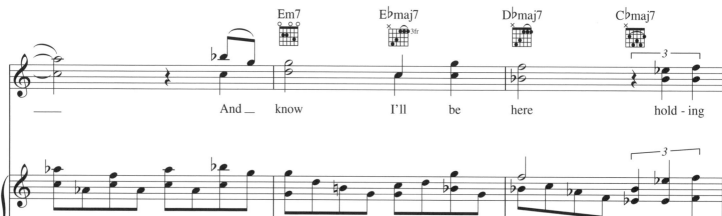

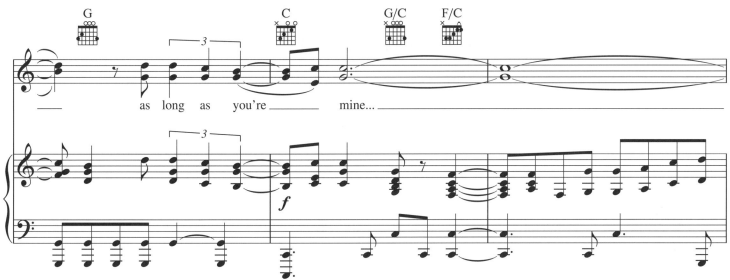

as long as you're _____ mine...

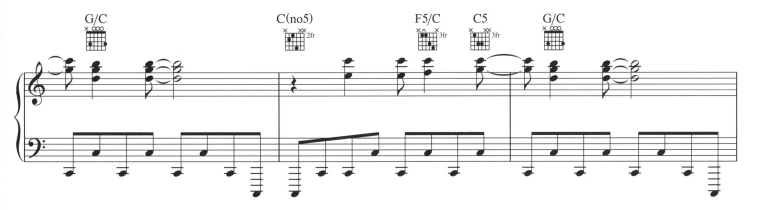

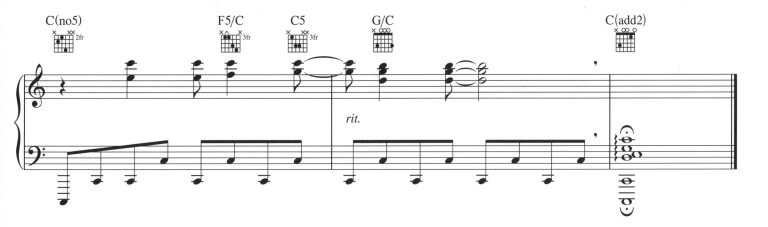

ALMOST PARADISE
from the Broadway Musical FOOTLOOSE

Words by DEAN PITCHFORD
Music by ERIC CARMEN

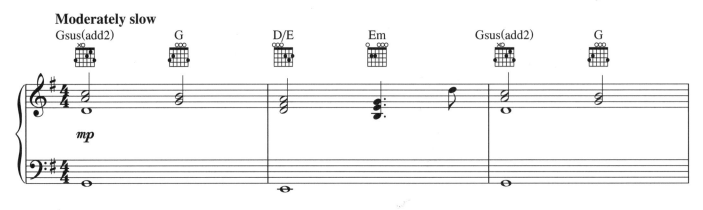

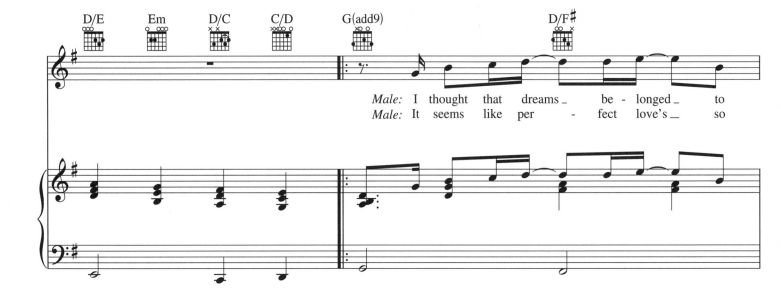

Male: I thought that dreams ___ be - longed ___ to
Male: It seems like per - fect love's ___ so

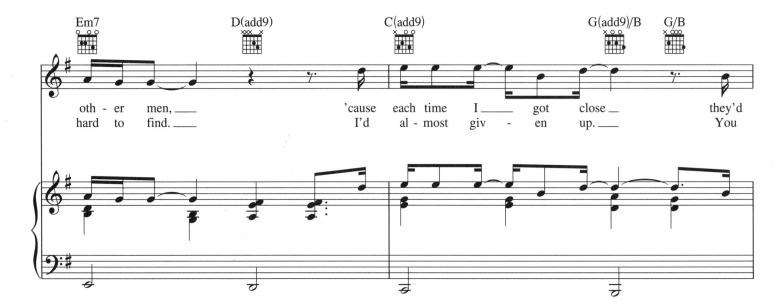

oth - er men, ___ 'cause each time I ___ got close ___ they'd
hard to find. ___ I'd al - most giv - en up. ___ You

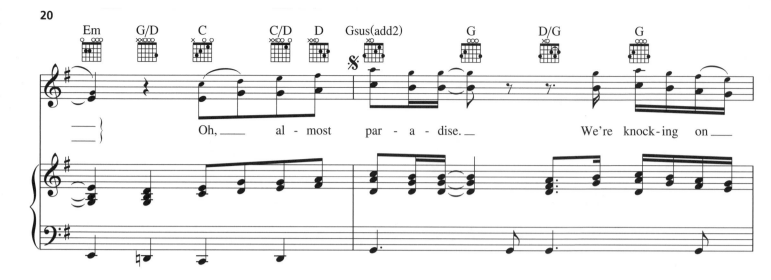

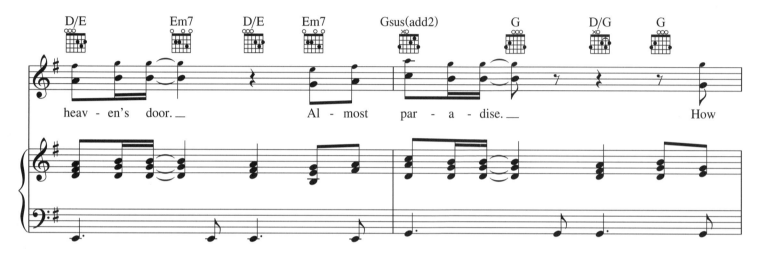

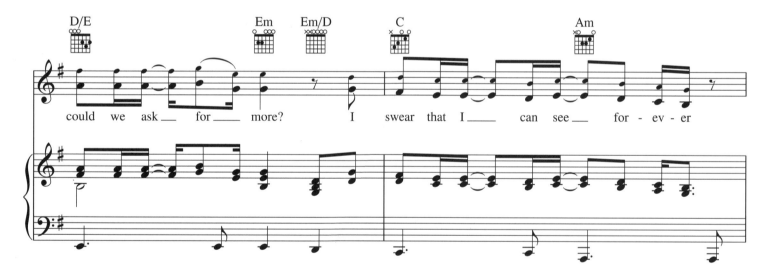

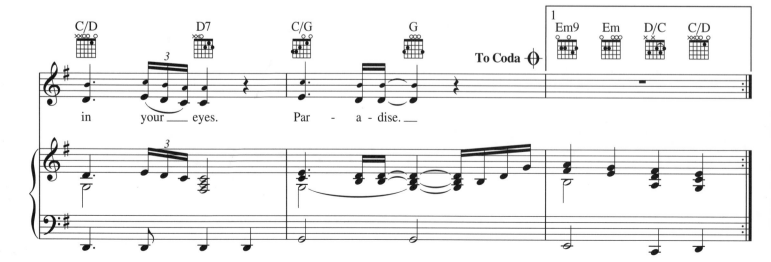

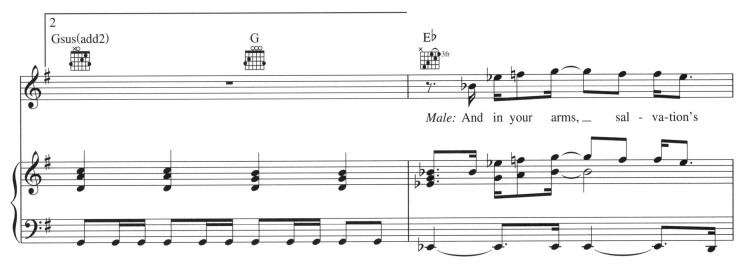

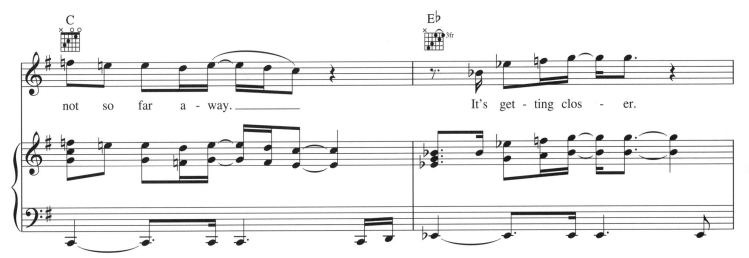

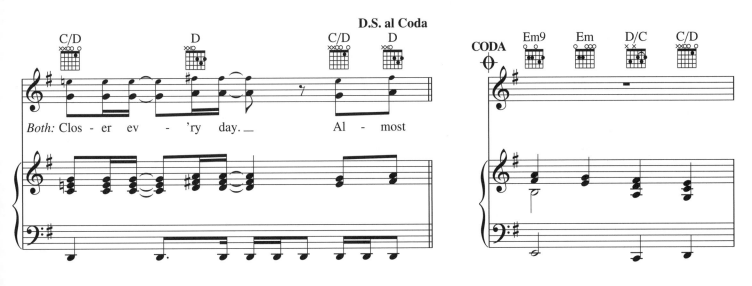

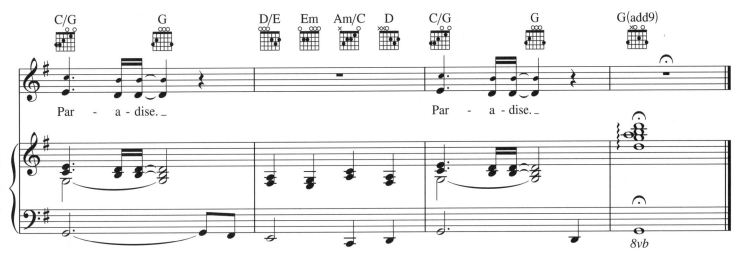

BEAUTY AND THE BEAST

from Walt Disney's BEAUTY AND THE BEAST: THE BROADWAY MUSICAL

Lyrics by HOWARD ASHMAN
Music by ALAN MENKEN

Lyrically

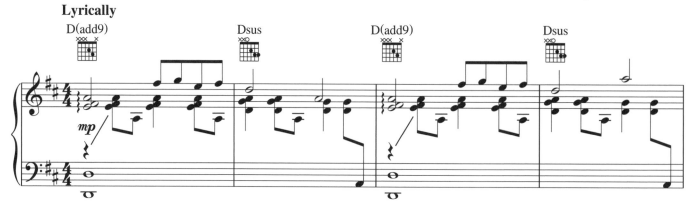

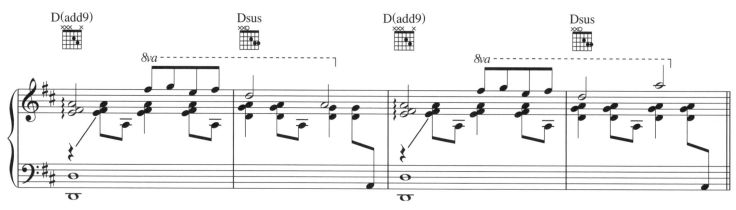

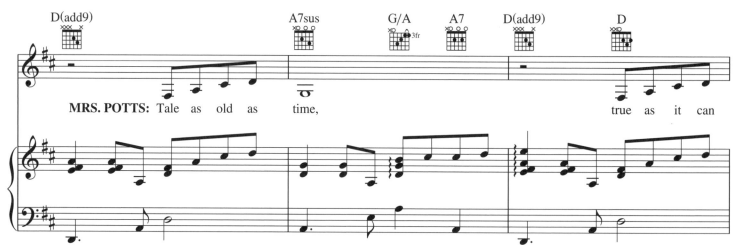

MRS. POTTS: Tale as old as time, true as it can be.

Bare-ly e-ven friends, then some-bod-y

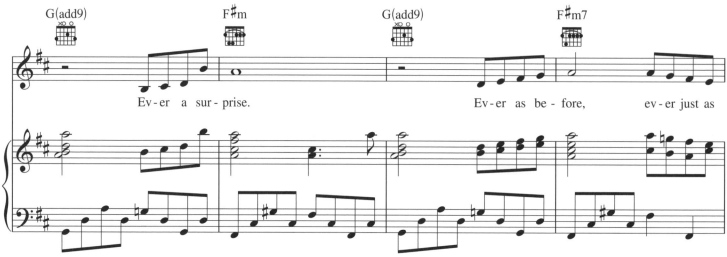

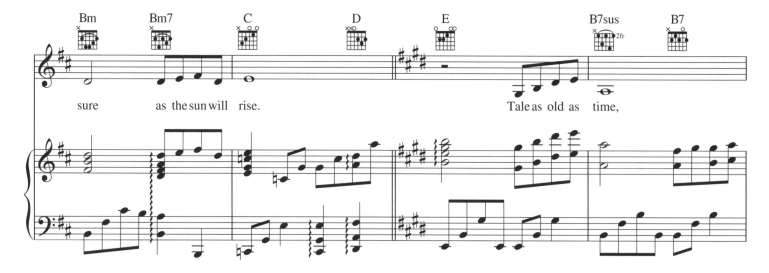

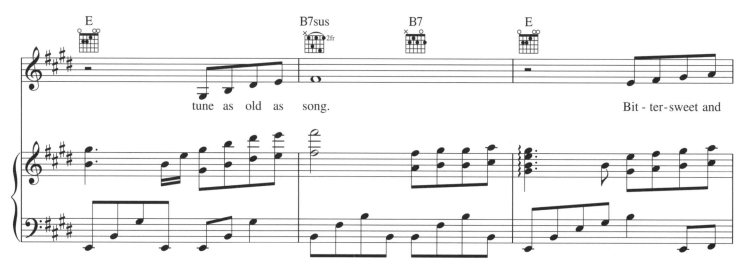

Can You Feel The Love Tonight

Disney Presents THE LION KING: THE BROADWAY MUSICAL

Music by ELTON JOHN
Lyrics by TIM RICE

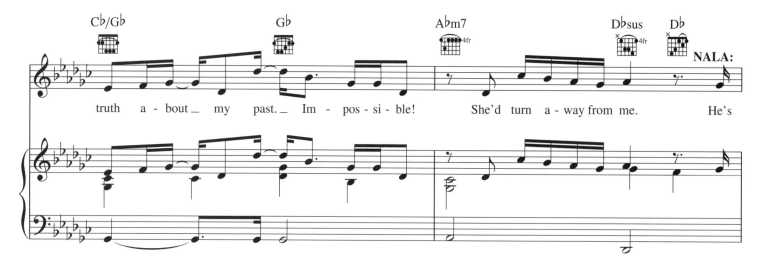

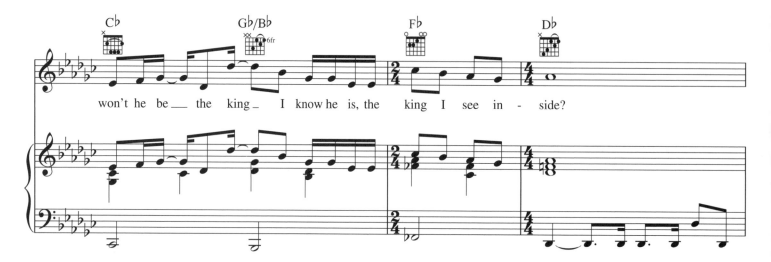

30

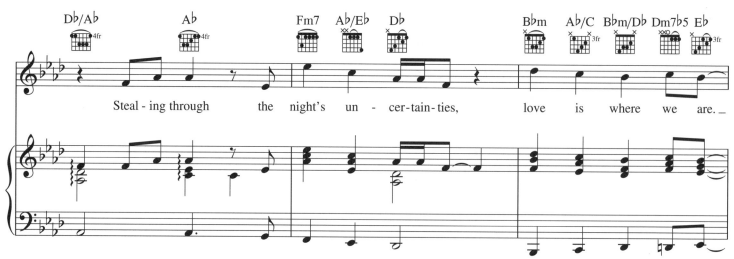

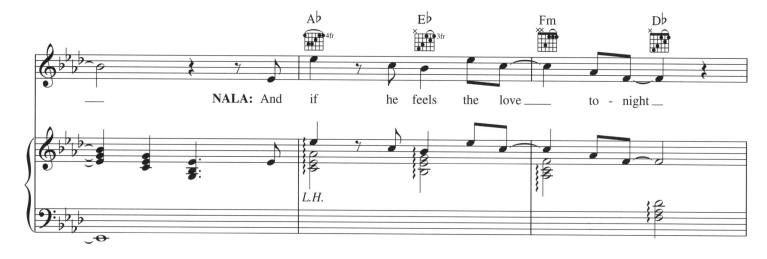

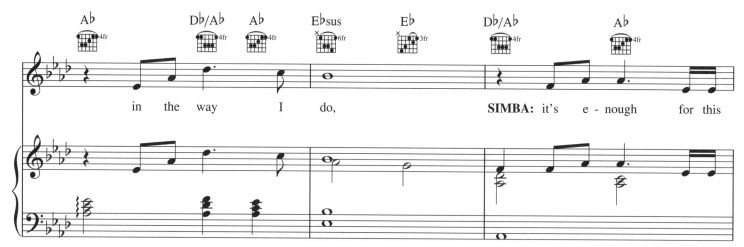

FOLLOW YOUR HEART
from URINETOWN

Music and Lyrics by MARK HOLLMANN
Book and Lyrics by GREG KOTIS

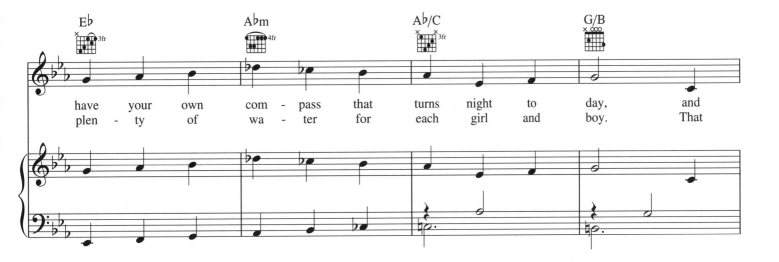

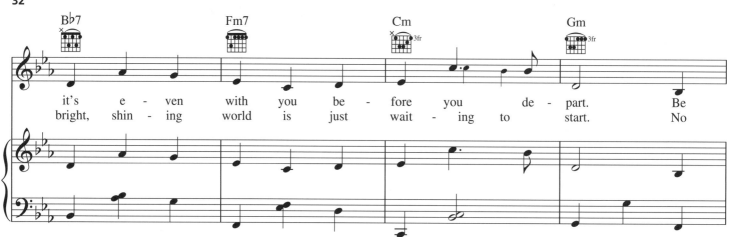

it's e - ven with you be - fore you de - part. Be

bright, shin - ing world is just wait - ing to start. No

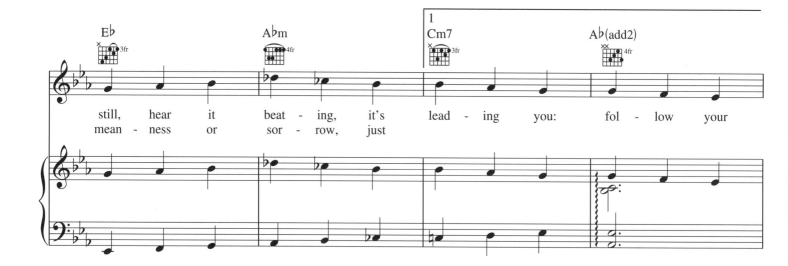

still, hear it beat - ing, it's lead - ing you: fol - low your

mean - ness or sor - row, just

heart. _____

rit.

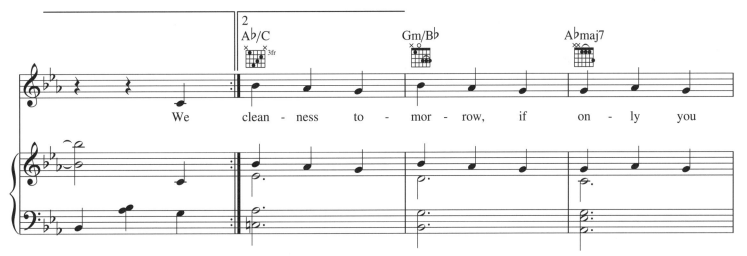

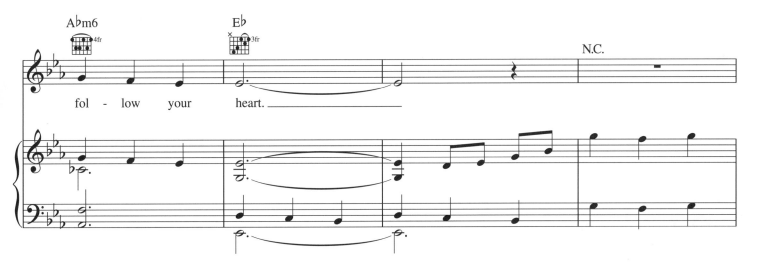

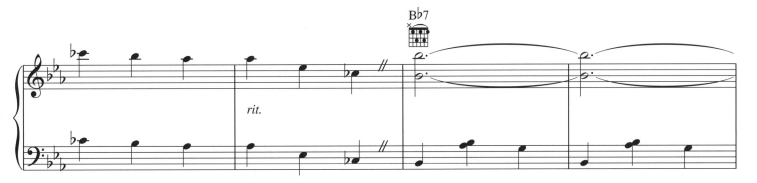

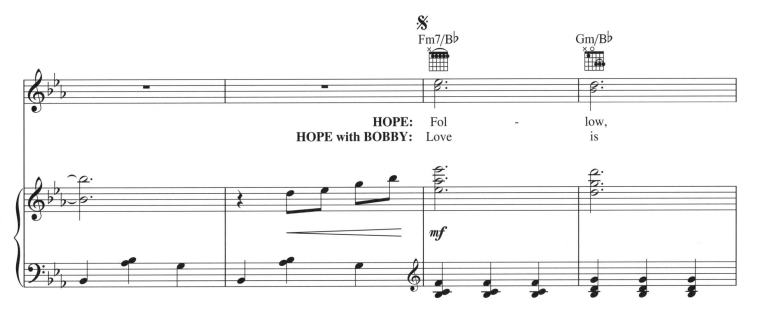

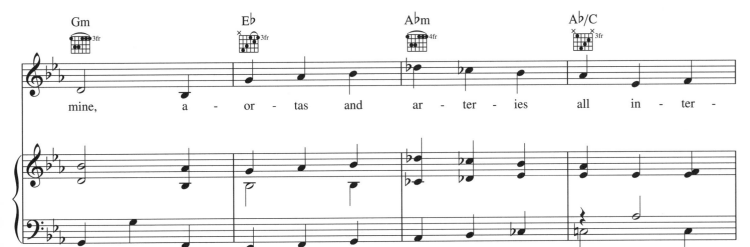

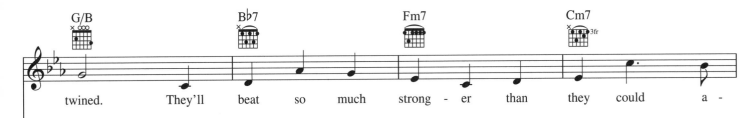

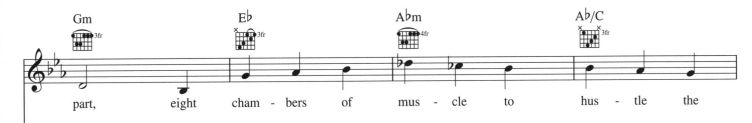

36

waiting to start. No anger or badness, just

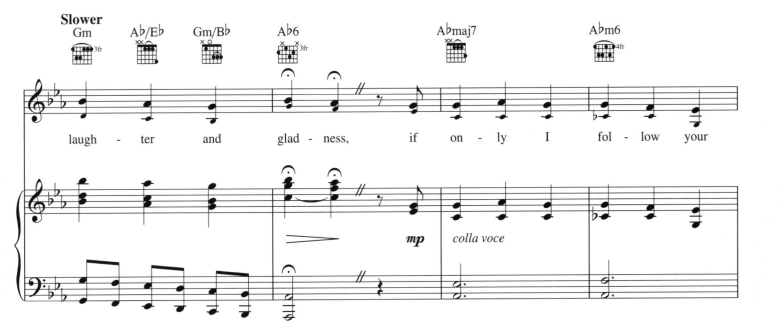

Slower

laughter and gladness, if only I follow your

mp *colla voce*

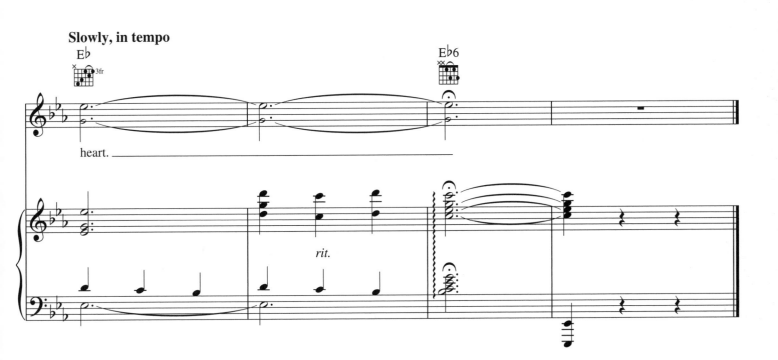

Slowly, in tempo

heart.

rit.

CAN'T TAKE MY EYES OFF OF YOU

Words and Music by BOB CREWE
and BOB GAUDIO

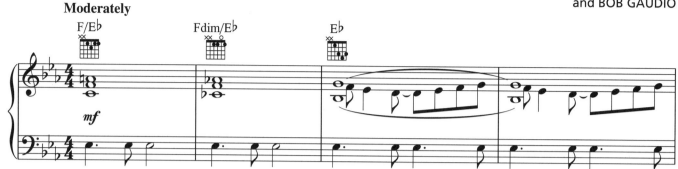

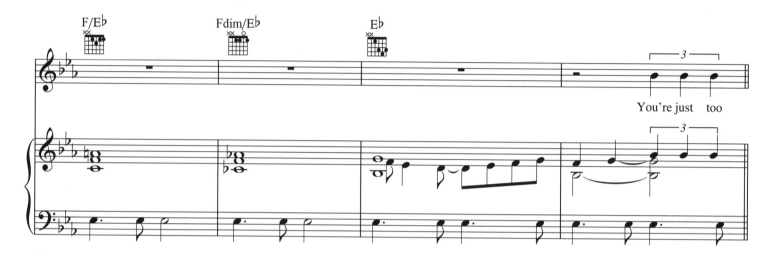

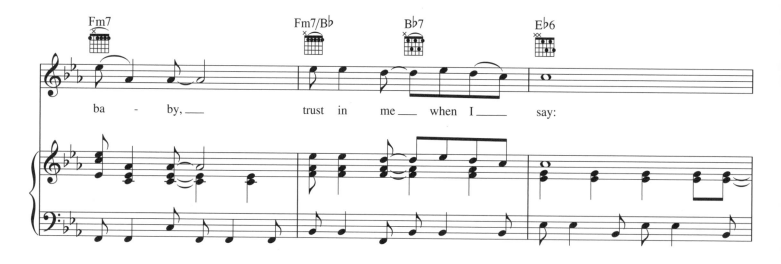

41

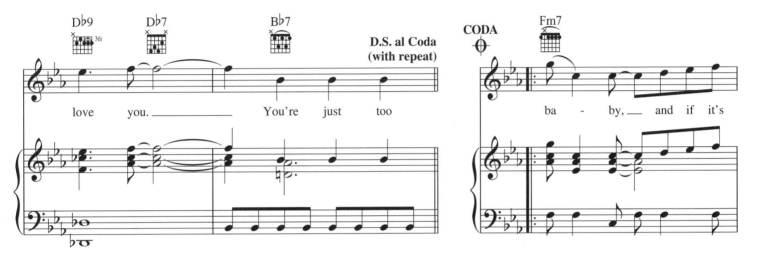

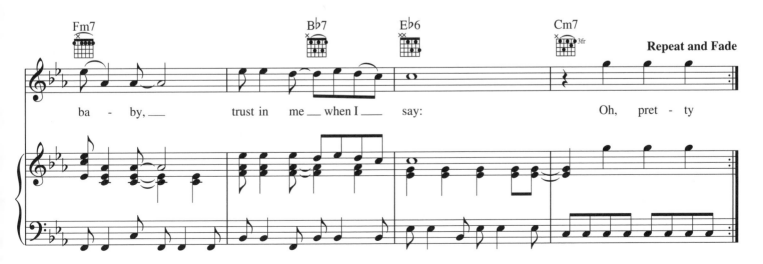

ELABORATE LIVES
from Elton John and Tim Rice's AIDA

Music by ELTON JOHN
Lyrics by TIM RICE

Moderately, with rubato

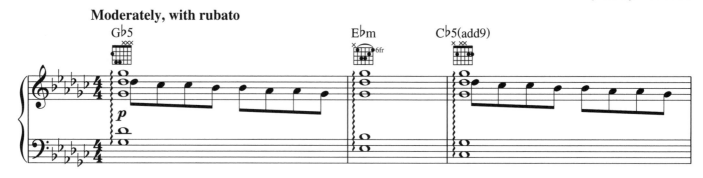

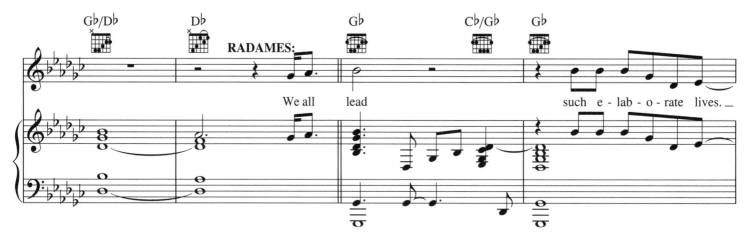

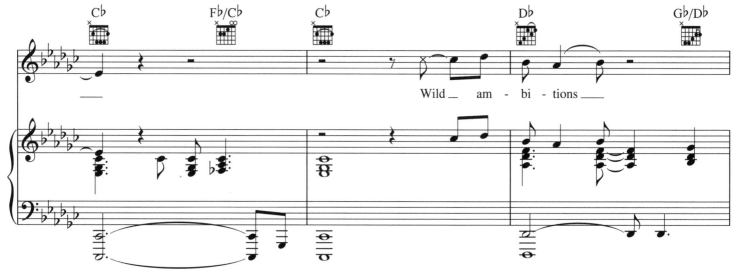

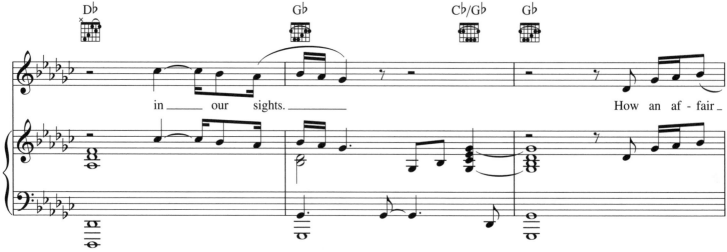

of the heart sur - vives. _____

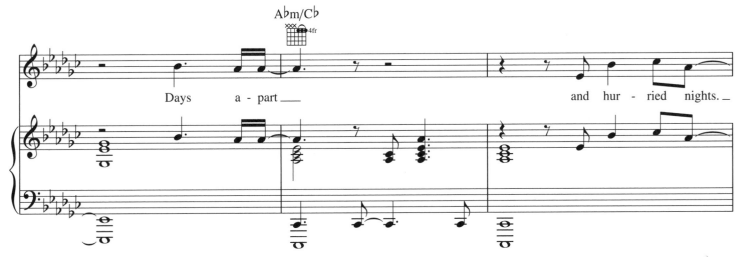

Days a - part _____ and hur - ried nights. __

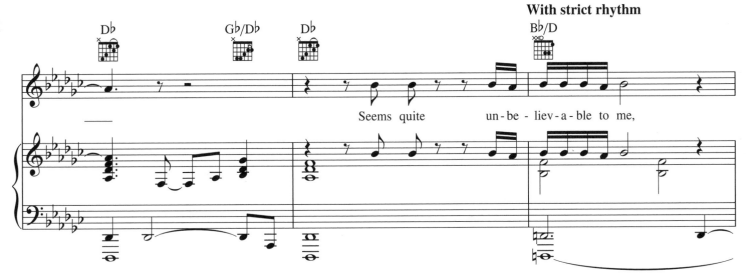

With strict rhythm

Seems quite un - be - liev - a - ble to me,

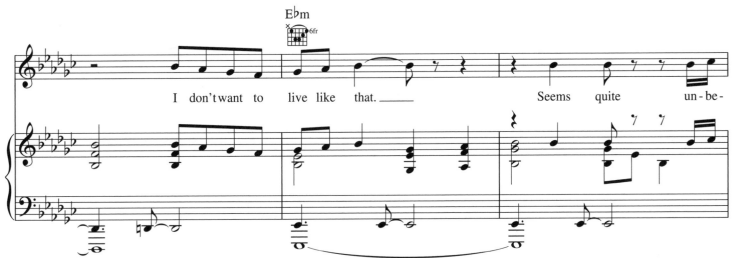

I don't want to live like that. _____ Seems quite un - be -

liev - a - ble to me, I don't want to love like that.

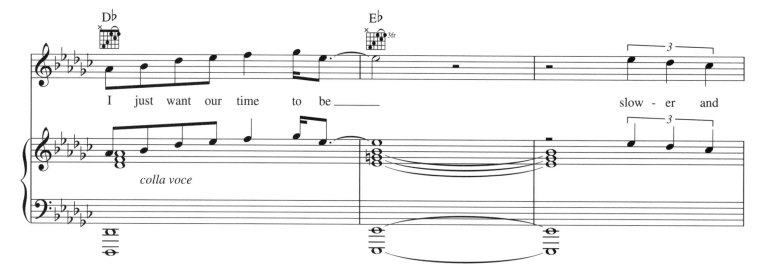

I just want our time to be _____ slow - er and

colla voce

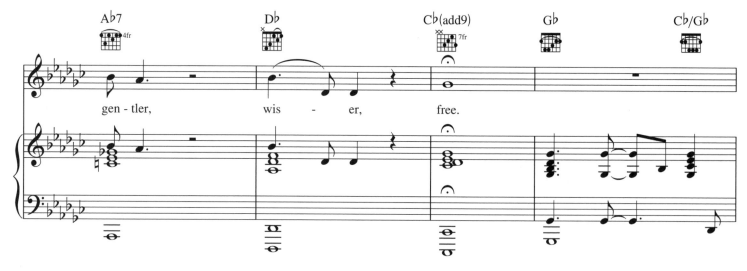

gen - tler, wis - er, free.

We all __ live _____ in ex - trav - a - gant times. __

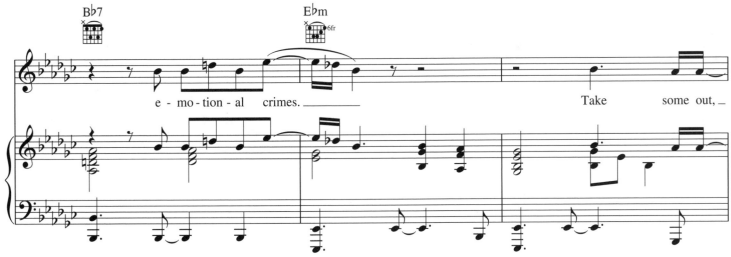

true. _____ This may not be the mo-ment

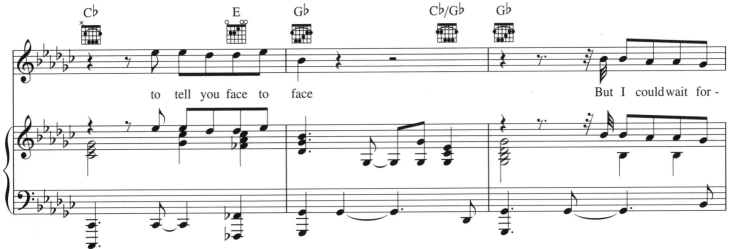

to tell you face to face   But I could wait for -

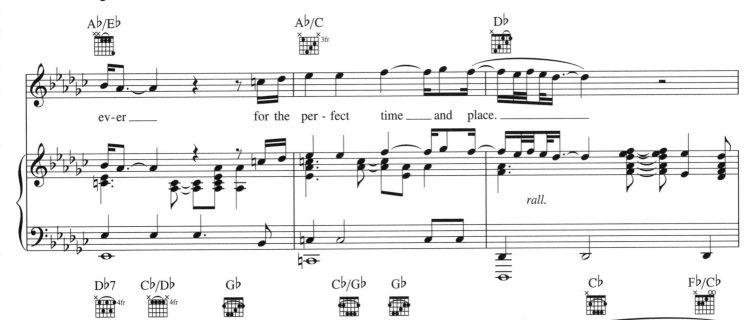

ev-er _____   for the per - fect   time _____ and place. _____

rall.

RADAMES:

AIDA: We all lead   such e - lab - o - rate lives. _____

a tempo

We don't know whose words are true. ___

Stran - gers, lov - ers, ___ hus - bands,

wives, ___ hard to know who's lov - ing ___

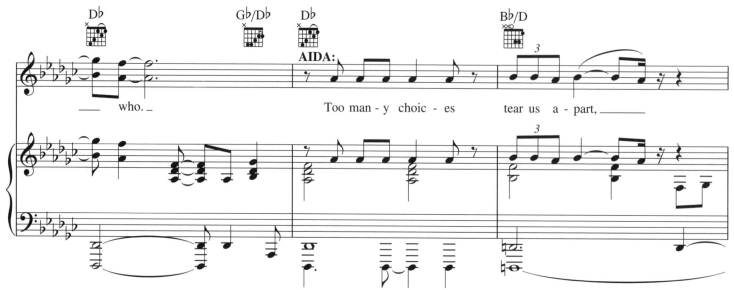

___ who. ___

AIDA: Too man - y choic - es tear us a - part, ___

A HEART FULL OF LOVE
from LES MISÉRABLES

Music by CLAUDE-MICHEL SCHÖNBERG
Lyrics by ALAIN BOUBLIL, JEAN-MARC NATEL and HERBERT KRETZMER

Allegretto

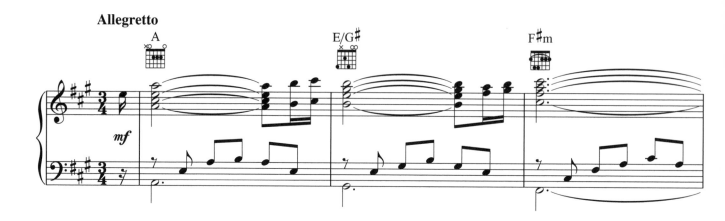

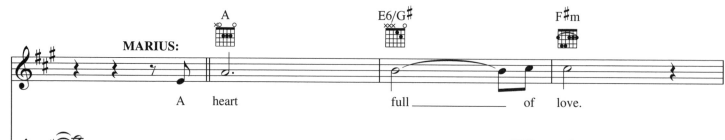

ev-'ry - thing all wrong! Oh God, for shame! I do not

e - ven __ know your name. Dear Mad' - moi - selle,

won't you say? No fear, heart

COSETTE:
(MARIUS:) Will you tell?

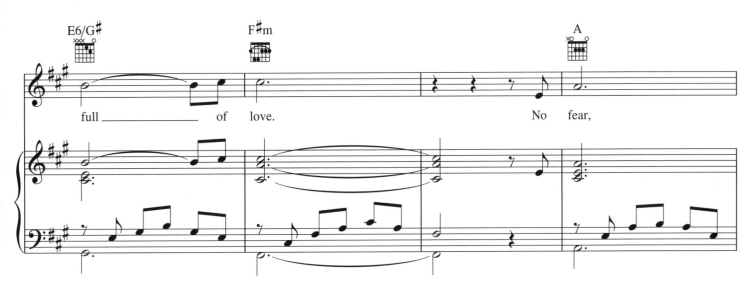

full __ of love. No fear,

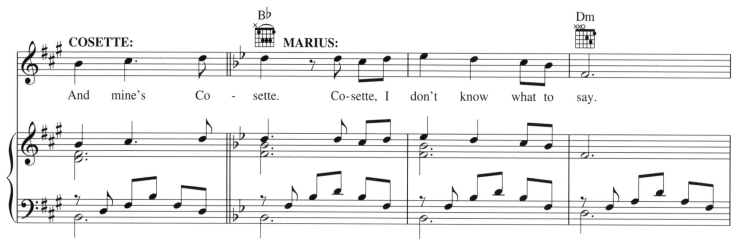

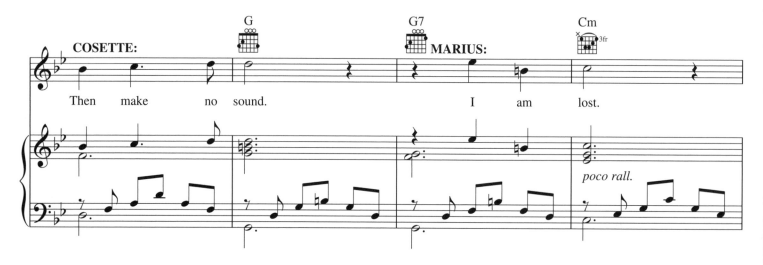

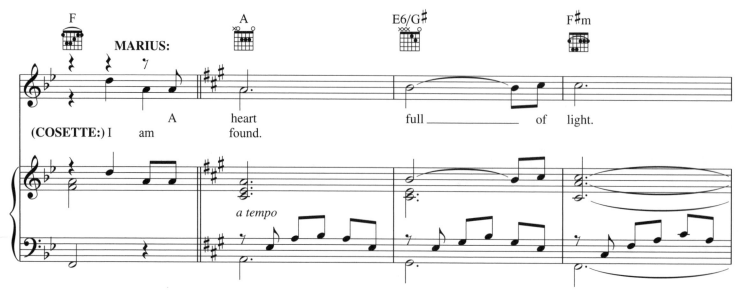

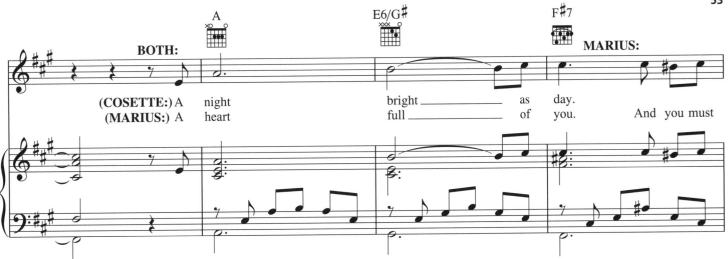

BOTH:
MARIUS:

(COSETTE:) A night   bright _____ as day.
(MARIUS:) A heart   full _____ of you.   And you must

nev - er go a - way.   Co - sette,   Co - sette,   this is a

chain we'll nev - er break.

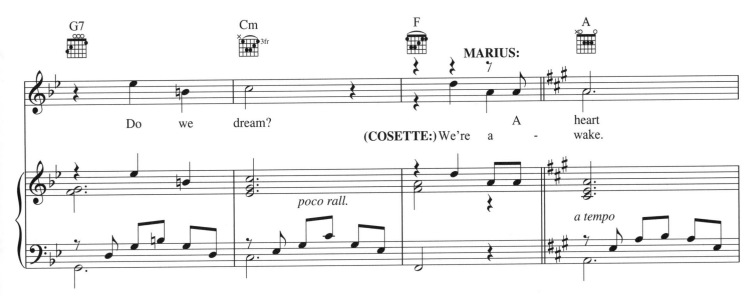

Do we dream?   A   heart

(COSETTE:) We're a - wake.

poco rall.

MARIUS:

a tempo

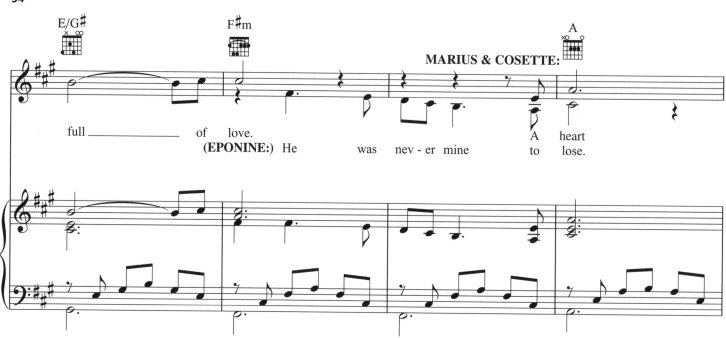

full _____ of love.

(EPONINE:) He was nev-er mine to lose.

MARIUS & COSETTE:

A heart

full _____ of you.

(EPONINE:) Why _____ re-gret what could not

MARIUS: A sin-gle look and ___ then I

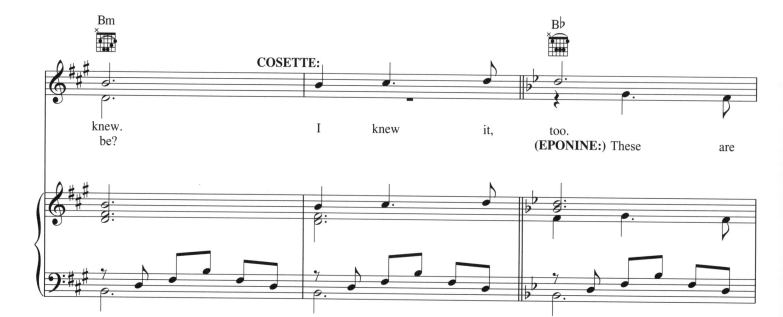

knew.
be?

COSETTE:

I knew it, too.

(EPONINE:) These are

I BELIEVE MY HEART
from THE WOMAN IN WHITE

Music by ANDREW LLOYD WEBBER
Lyrics by DAVID ZIPPEL

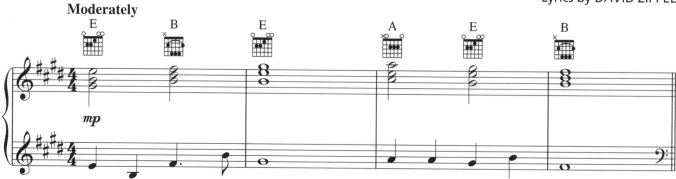

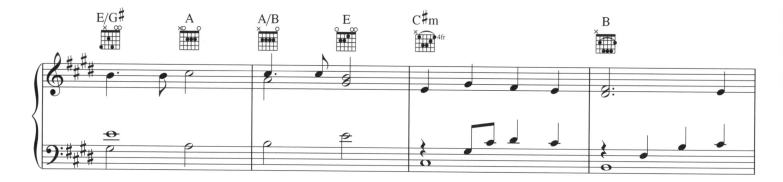

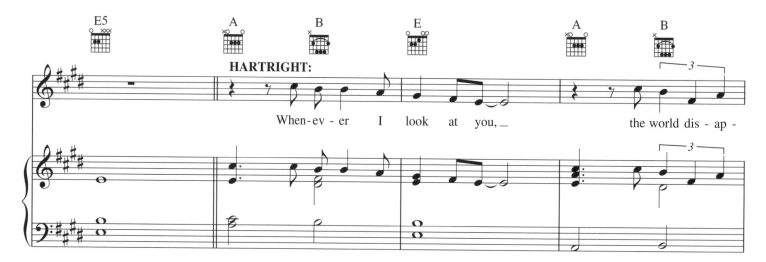

HARTRIGHT:

When-ev - er I look at you, _ the world dis - ap -

pears. All in a sin - gle glance so re - veal - ing. _____

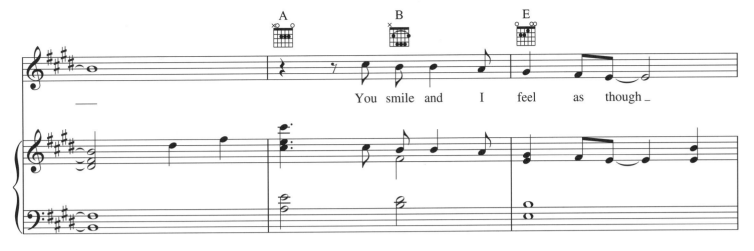

You smile and I feel as though_

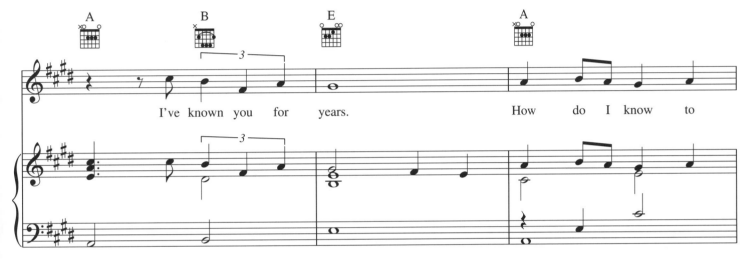

I've known you for years. How do I know to

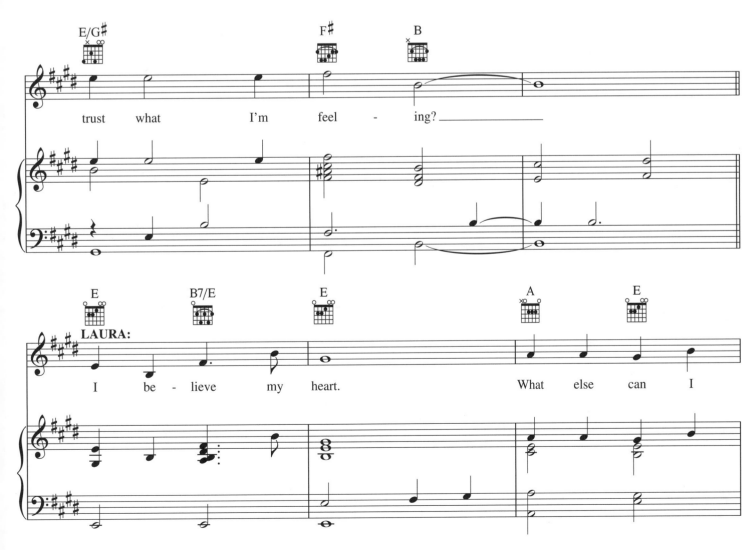

trust what I'm feel - ing?___

LAURA:

I be - lieve my heart. What else can I

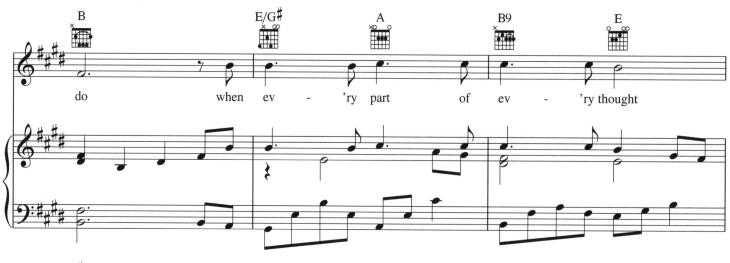

do   when ev - 'ry part   of ev - 'ry thought

HARTRIGHT:

leads me straight to you?   I be - lieve my heart.

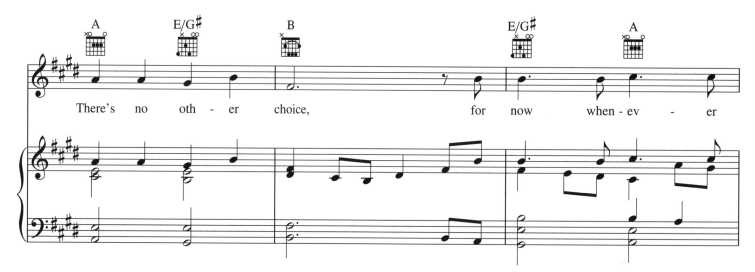

There's no oth - er choice,   for now when - ev - er

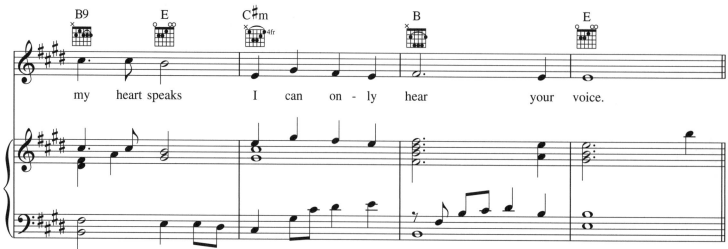

my heart speaks I can on - ly hear   your voice.

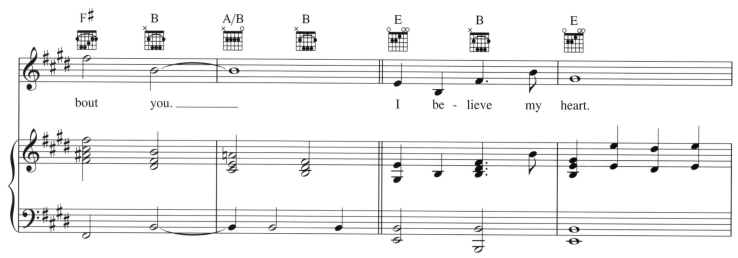

bout you. _____ I be - lieve my heart.

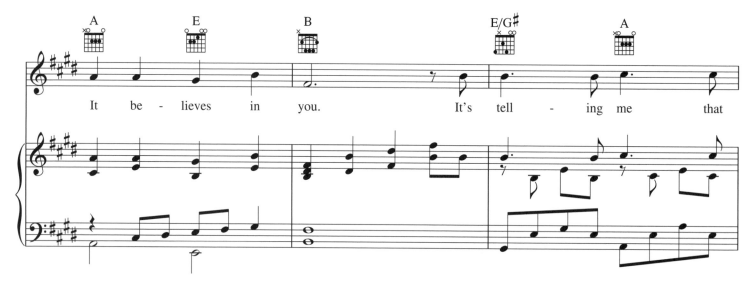

It be - lieves in you. It's tell - ing me that

what I see is com - plete - ly true.

LAURA:

I be - lieve my heart. How can it be

wrong? It says that what I feel for you,

I will feel my whole life long.

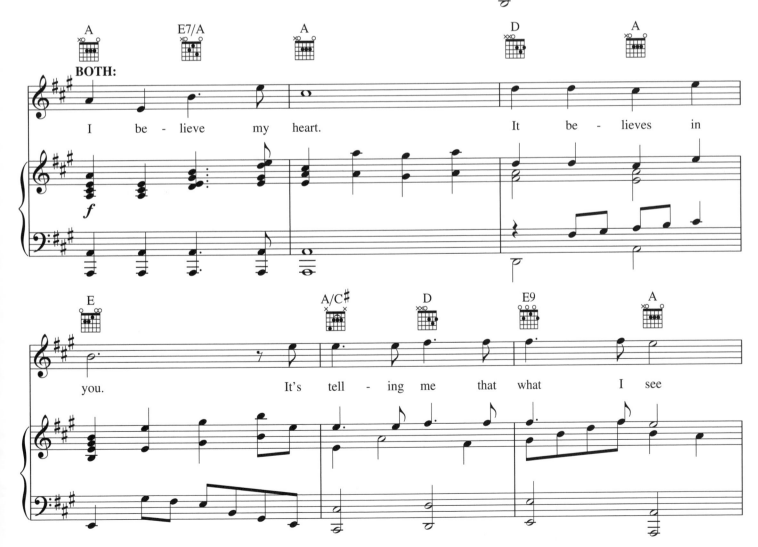

BOTH:

I be - lieve my heart. It be - lieves in you.

you. It's tell - ing me that what I see

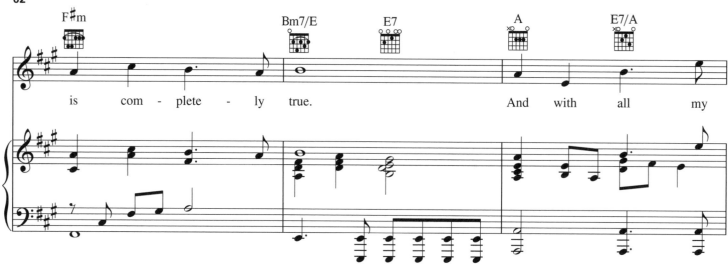

is com - plete - ly true. And with all my

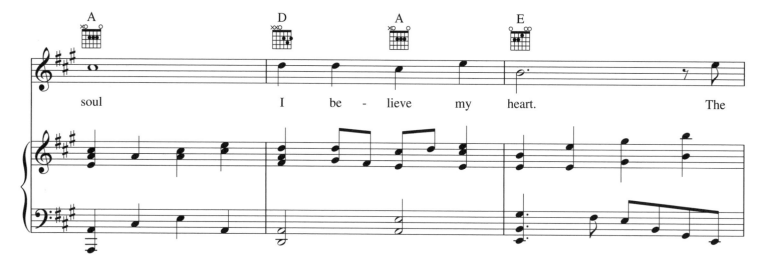

soul I be - lieve my heart. The

por - trait that it paints of you is a per - fect

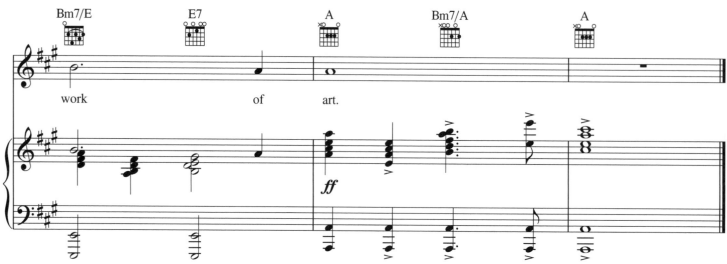

work of art.

JUST THE WAY YOU ARE

featured in MOVIN' OUT

Words and Music by
BILLY JOEL

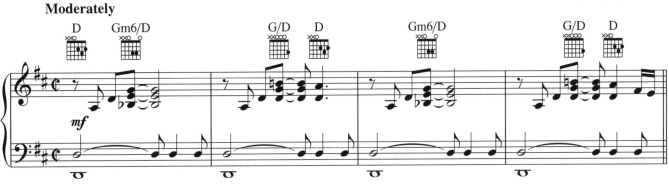

Don't go chang-ing _____ to try and please me. _____

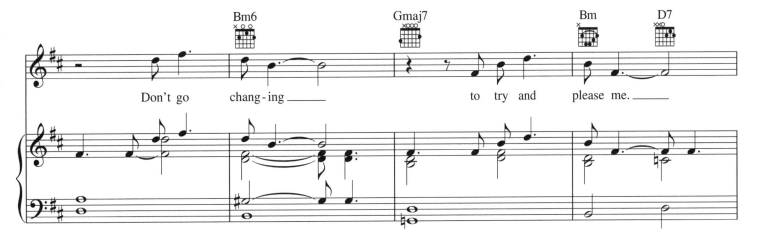

You nev-er let me down _ be-fore. _____ Mm, _____ mm.

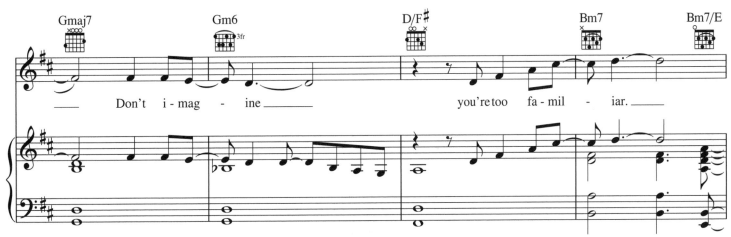

_____ Don't i-mag-ine _____ you're too fa-mil-iar. _____

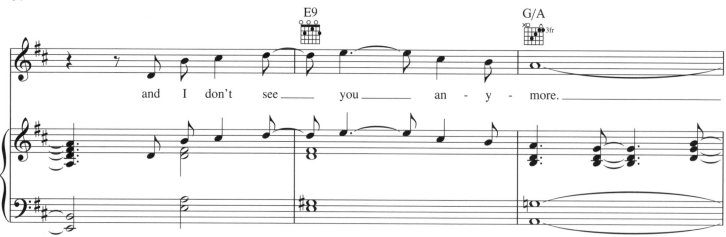

and I don't see _____ you _____ an - y - more. _____

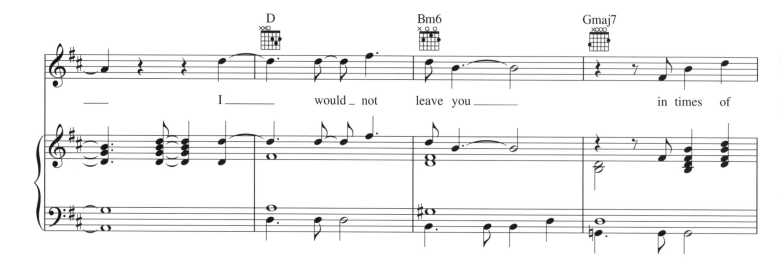

_____ I _____ would _ not leave you _____ in times of

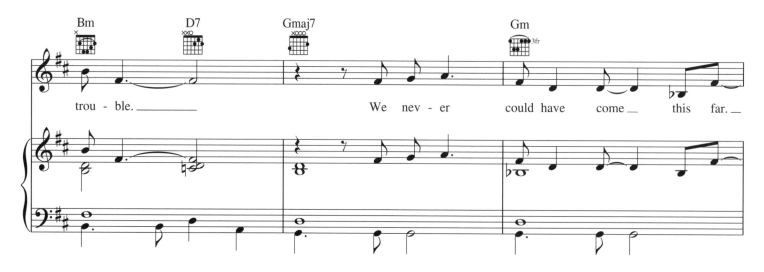

trou - ble. _____ We nev - er could have come _ this far. _

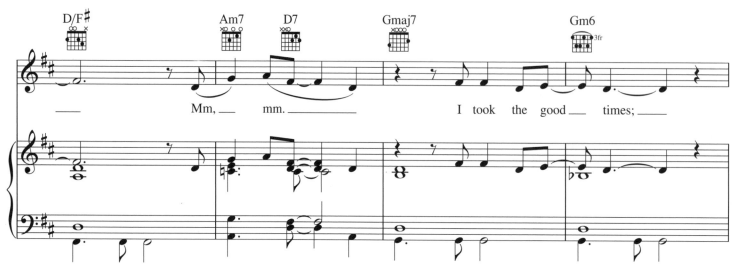

_____ Mm, _ mm. _____ I took the good _ times; _

I'll take the bad __ times. __ I'll take you just __

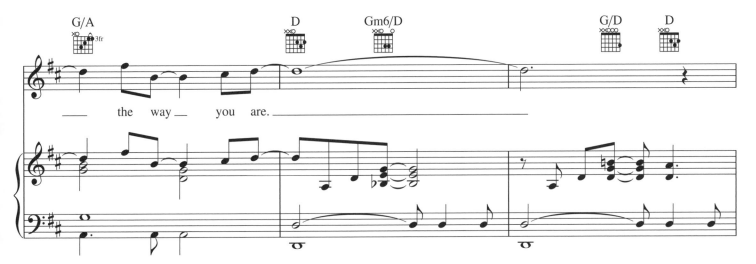

__ the way __ you are. __

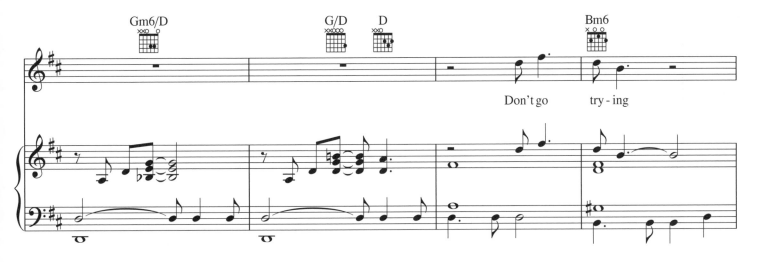

Don't go try - ing

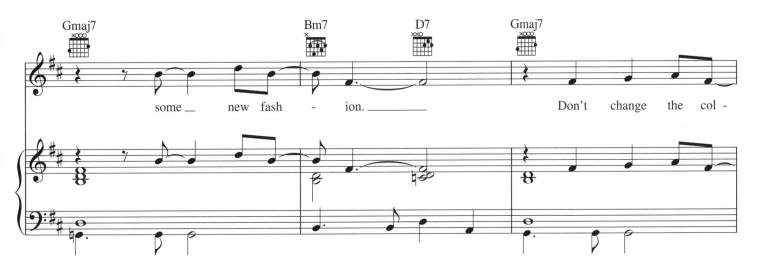

some __ new fash - ion. __ Don't change the col -

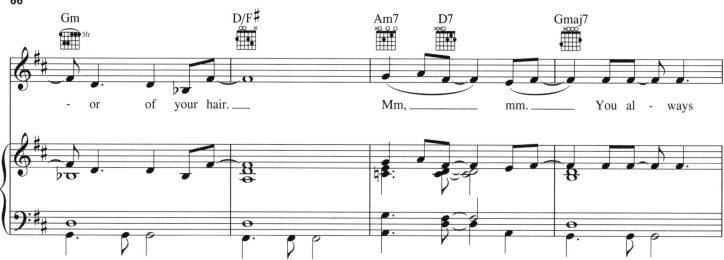

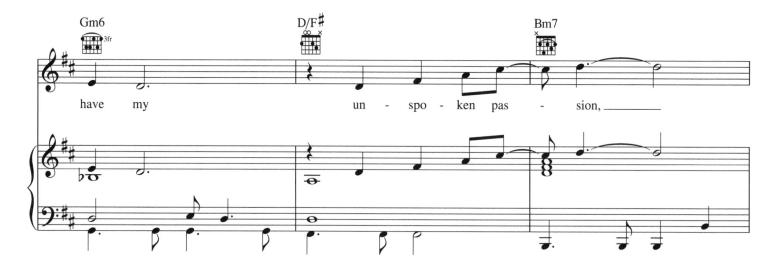

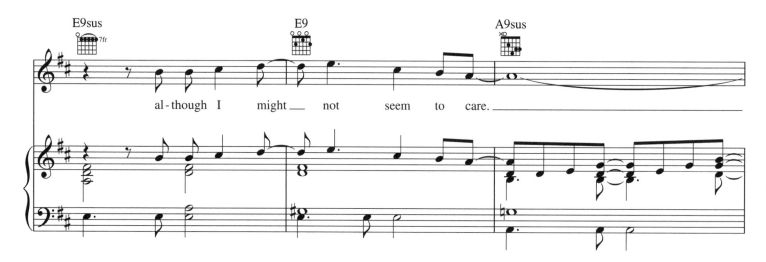

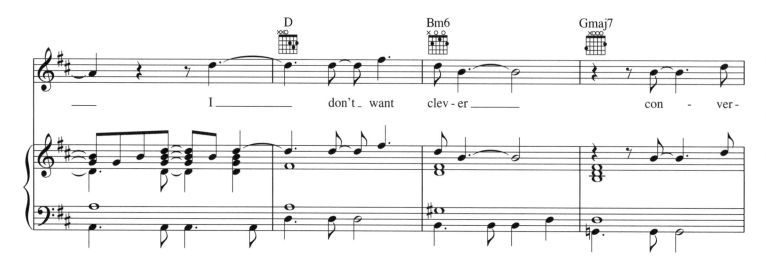

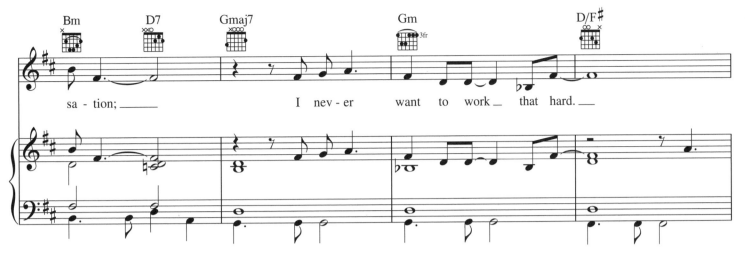

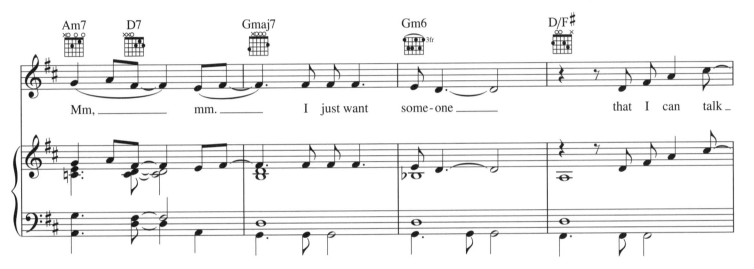

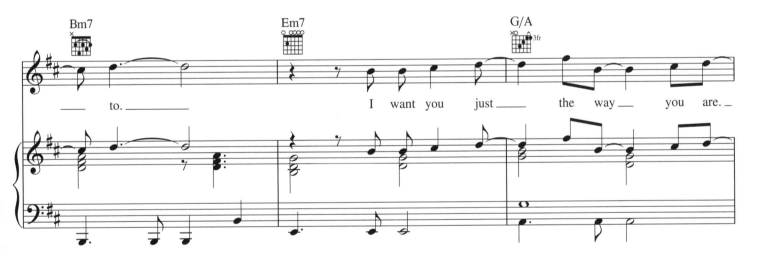

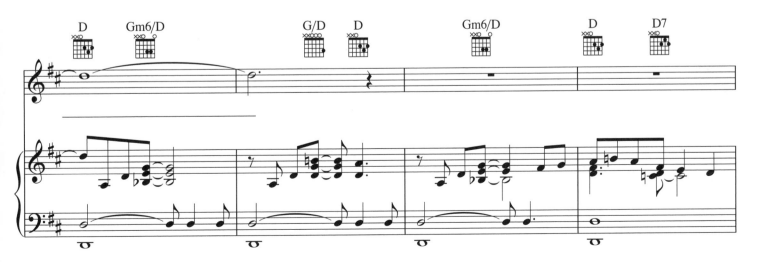

I need to know___ that you___ will al - ways be___

the same old some - one that I knew.___ Oh,

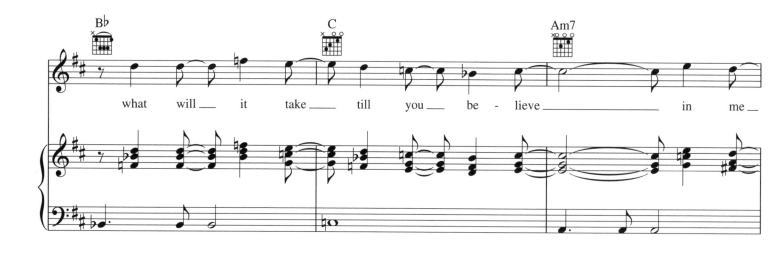

what will___ it take___ till you___ be - lieve_____ in me___

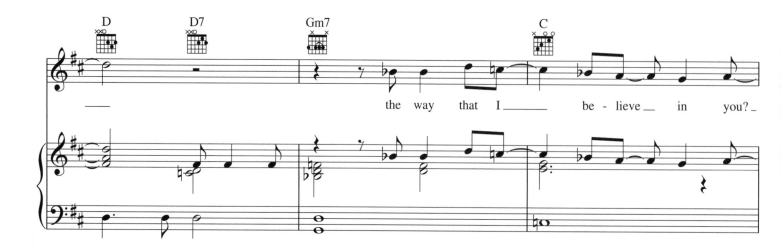

___ the way that I_____ be - lieve___ in you?___

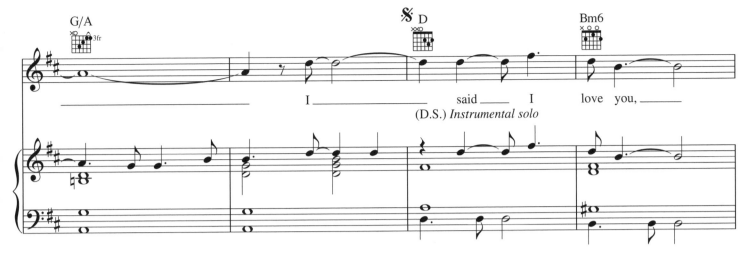

I _____ said ___ I love you, _____
(D.S.) *Instrumental solo*

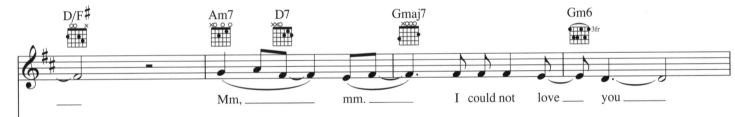

and that's for - ev - er, _____ and this I prom - ise from the heart. _

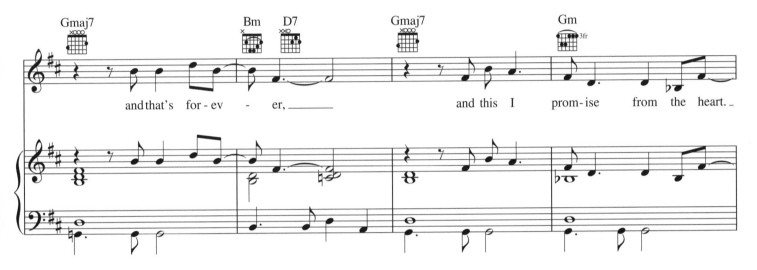

Mm, _____ mm. _____ I could not love ___ you _____

To Coda ⊕

an - y ___ bet - ter. _____ I love you just _

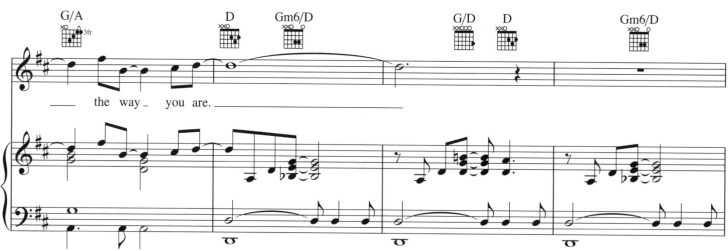

the way you are.

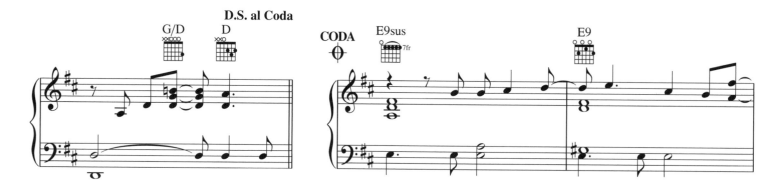

D.S. al Coda

CODA

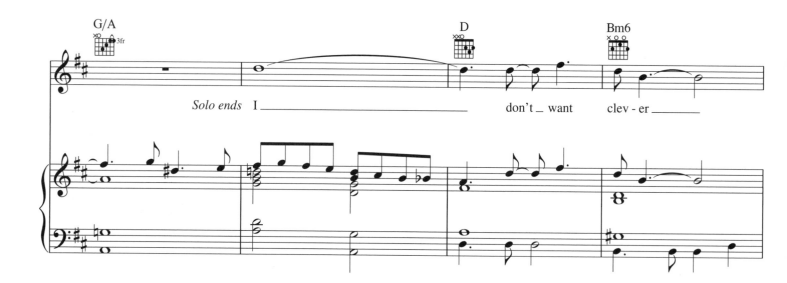

Solo ends I don't want clev-er

con - ver - sa - tion; I nev-er

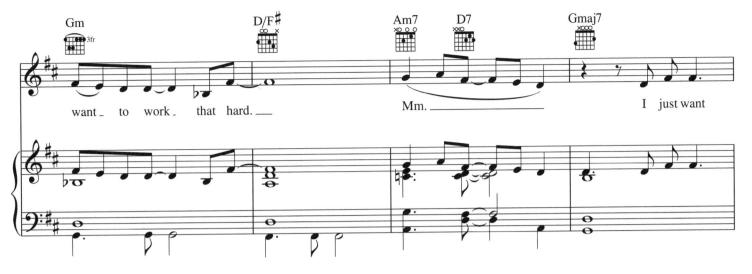

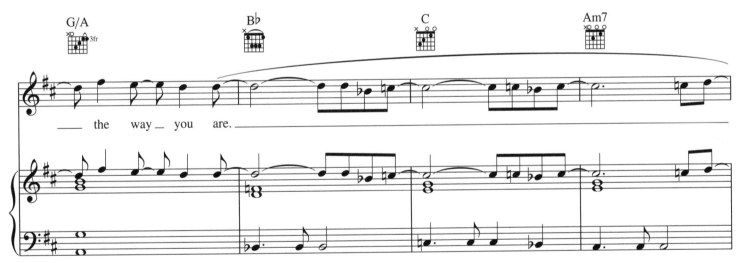

THE LAST NIGHT OF THE WORLD

from MISS SAIGON

Music by CLAUDE-MICHEL SCHÖNBERG
Lyrics by RICHARD MALTBY JR. and ALAIN BOUBLIL
Adapted from original French Lyrics by ALAIN BOUBLIL

Languidly

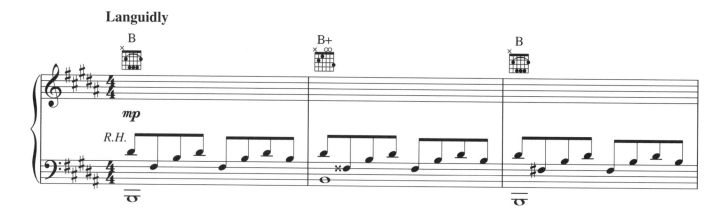

CHRIS: In a place that won't let us feel, ___

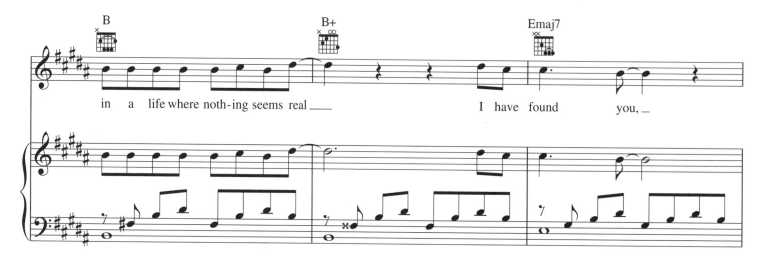

in a life where noth-ing seems real ___ I have found you, _

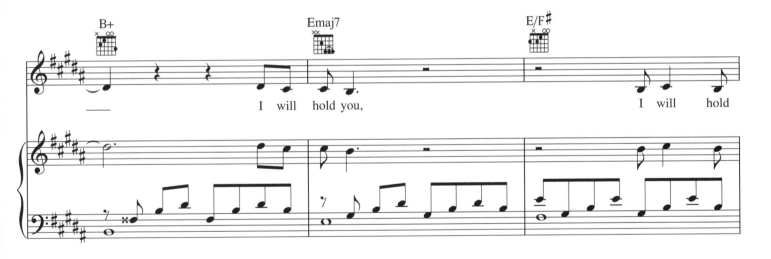

hearts dream the dis - tant drums. _____ And we have

CHRIS:

mu - sic al - right __ tear - ing the night. _ A song

rit. *a tempo*

played on a so - lo sax - o - phone. __ A

cra - zy sound, _ a lone - ly sound, _ a cry that tells us love _

CHRIS:

KIM:

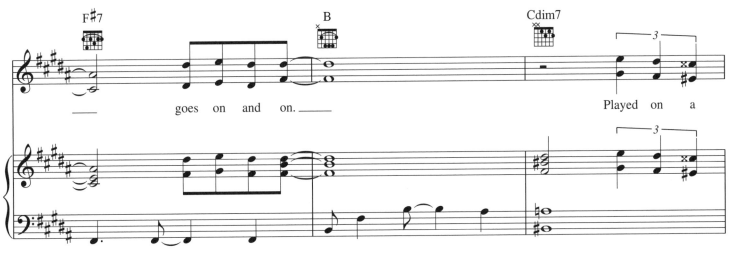

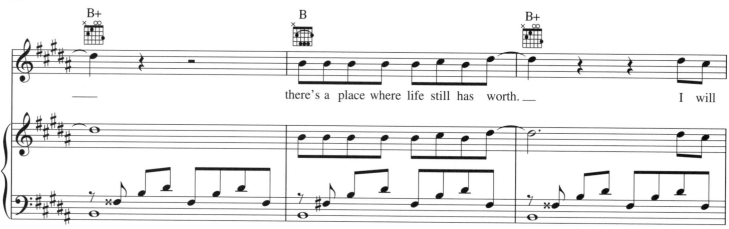

there's a place where life still has worth. __ I will

take you. KIM: I'll go with you. __ CHRIS: You won't be -

lieve all the things you'll see. __ I know 'cause you'll see them all with me. __

CHRIS:

KIM:

__ If we're to - geth - er, well then, we'll hear it a - gain, a

song played on a so - lo sax - o - phone.

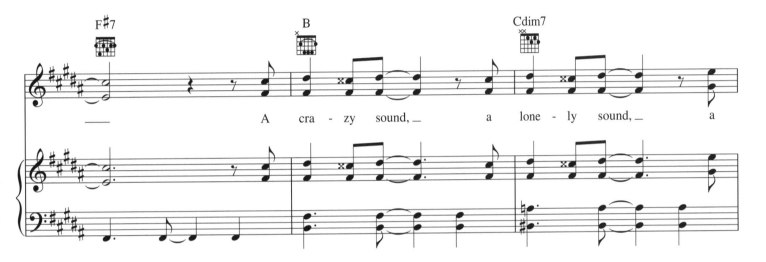

A cra - zy sound, __ a lone - ly sound, __ a

cry that tells us love __ goes on and on. __

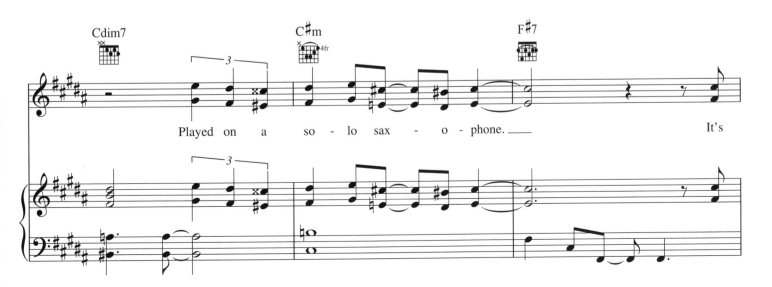

Played on a so - lo sax - o - phone. __ It's

tell - ing me ___ to hold you tight ___ and dance like it's the last ___

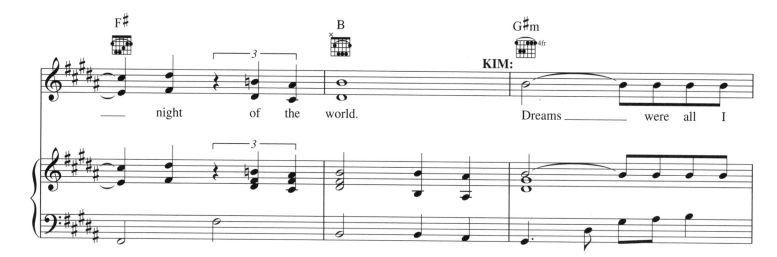

___ night of the world. Dreams ___ were all I

KIM:

ev - er knew. ___ Dreams ___ you won't need when I'm through. ___

CHRIS:

An - y-where we may be I will sing ___ with

BOTH:

CHRIS:

KIM:

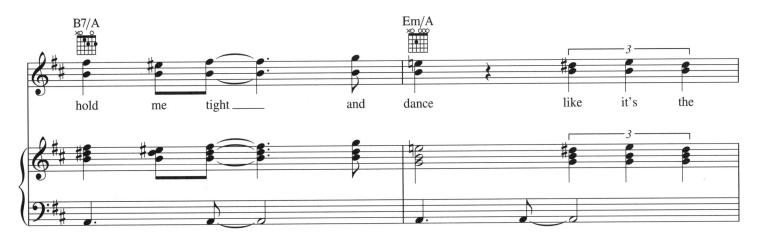

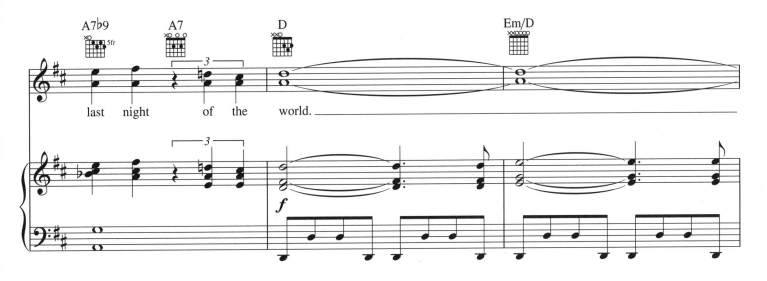

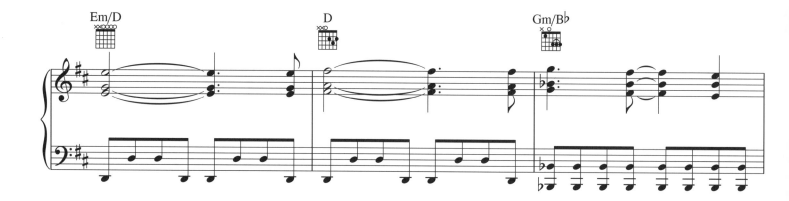

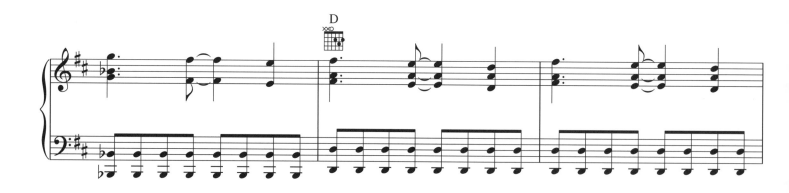

LOVE CHANGES EVERYTHING
from ASPECTS OF LOVE

Music by ANDREW LLOYD WEBBER
Lyrics by DON BLACK and CHARLES HART

Drammatico

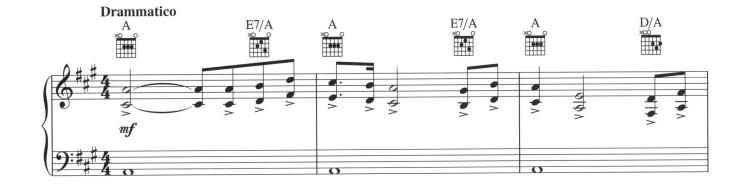

Love, love chang-es ev-'ry-thing: hands and
Love, love chang-es ev-'ry-thing: days are

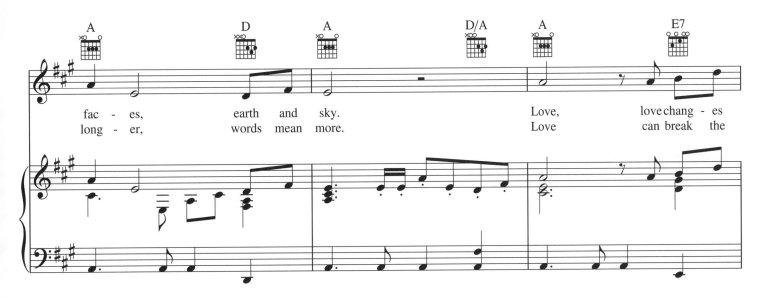

fac-es, earth and sky. Love, love chang-es
long-er, words mean more. Love can break the

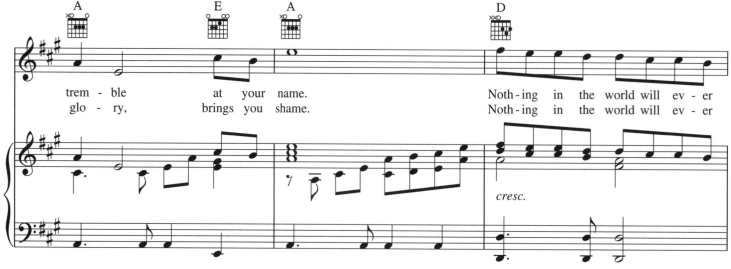

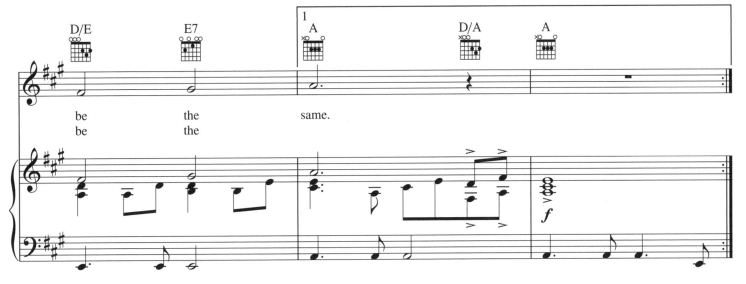

be   the   same.
be   the

same. _____

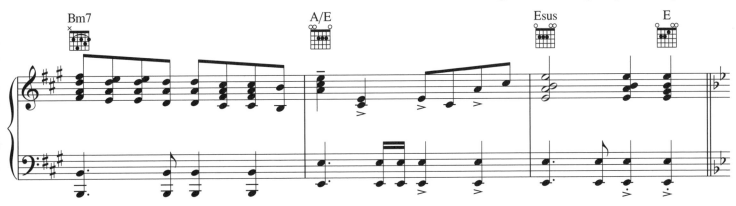

Off _____ in - to the world we go,   plan -ning fu - tures,   shap -ing

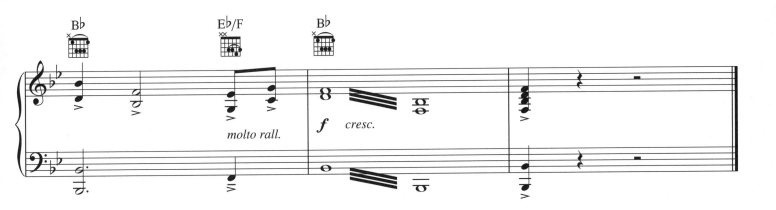

LOVE SNEAKS IN
from DIRTY ROTTEN SCOUNDRELS

Words and Music by
DAVID YAZBEK

LAWRENCE:
Love sneaks in when ev-'ry-thing seems qui - et.

Sets the bait __ and like a fool __ you buy it. Your fa-mous self-pos-ses - sion's van-ished

from your re-per-toire. __ This is what __ can hap-pen when you leave the door __ a-jar. And

LOVE TO ME

from THE LIGHT IN THE PIAZZA

Words and Music by
ADAM GUETTEL

Tenderly

FABRIZIO:

The day we meet, the way you

lean a - gainst the wind   and do not

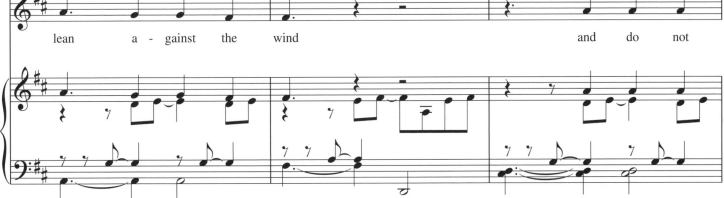

know that you are beau - ti - ful,

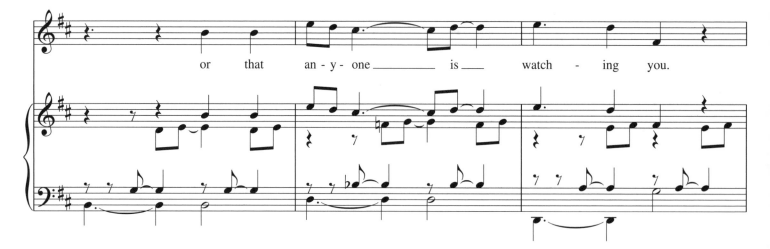

or that an-y-one _____ is ____ watch - ing you.

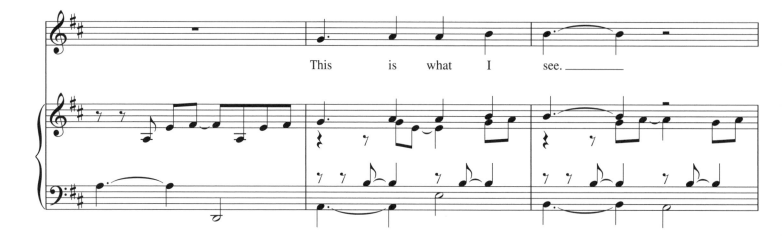

This is what I see. _____

And I

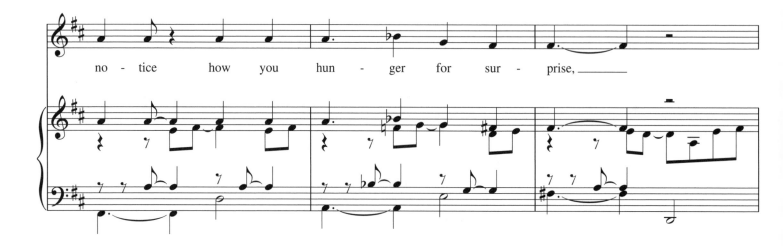

no - tice how you hun - ger for sur - prise, _____

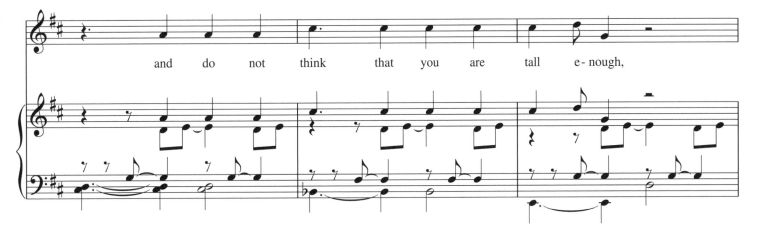

and do not think that you are tall e- nough,

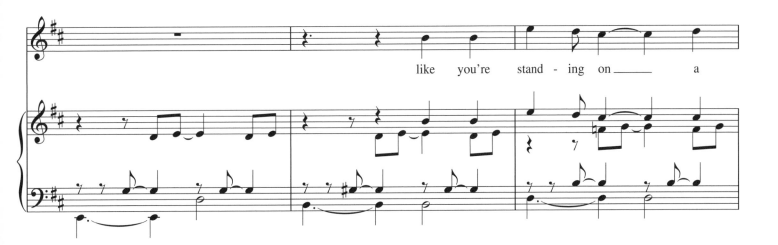

like you're stand - ing on _____ a

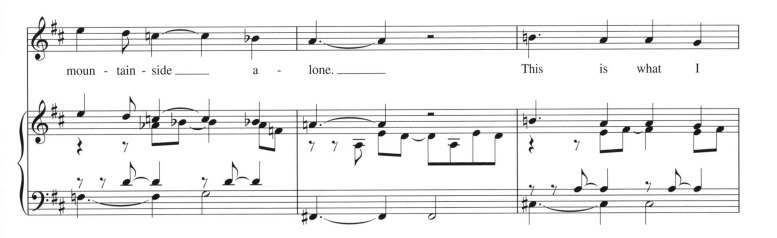

moun - tain - side _____ a - lone. _____ This is what I

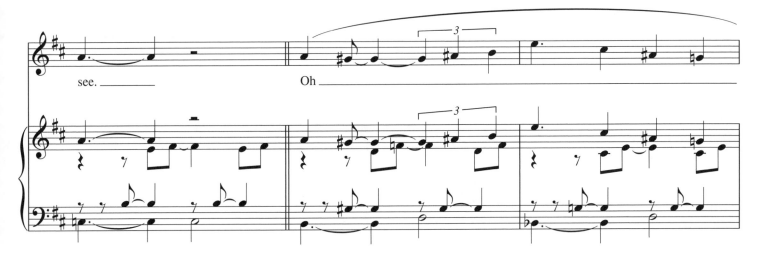

see. _____ Oh _____

92

Oh

You're not _____ a - lone! _____

Now I see as I have nev-er seen _____ be -

fore, _____ since that mo - ment in the square _____

when your hat is car - ried in the air____

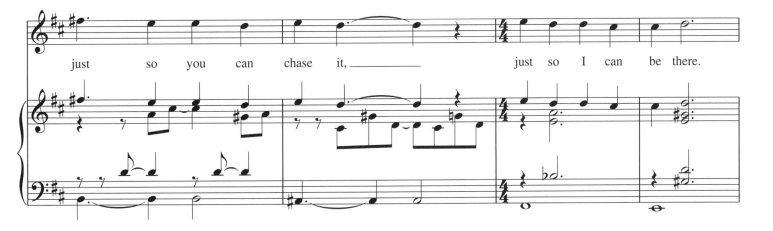

just so you can chase it,_____ just so I can be there.

This is how I know. This is what I see. This is love to me._____

rit.

ONCE YOU LOSE YOUR HEART

from ME AND MY GIRL

Words and Music by
NOEL GAY

out love, _____ and all the joy that love a - lone can bring.

All that I have ev - er learnt a - bout love, _____ tells me it's a ver - y fun - ny

thing. For when your heart is fan - cy free, you hope some man will choose it, but

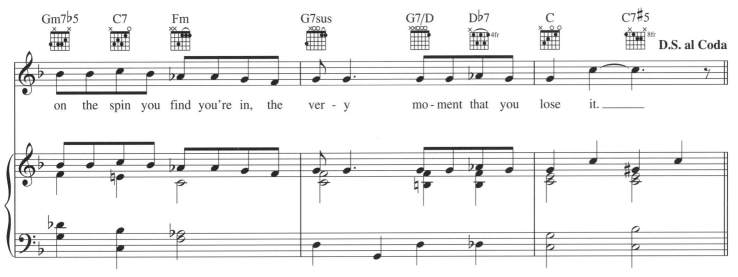

D.S. al Coda

on the spin you find you're in, the ver-y mo-ment that you lose it. _____

CODA

there's one thing cer-tain from the start, _____ you've got to fol - low, you've got to

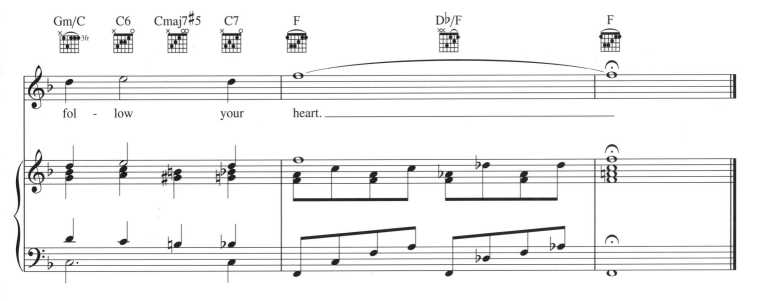

fol - low your heart. _____

SEASONS OF LOVE

from RENT

Words and Music by
JONATHAN LARSON

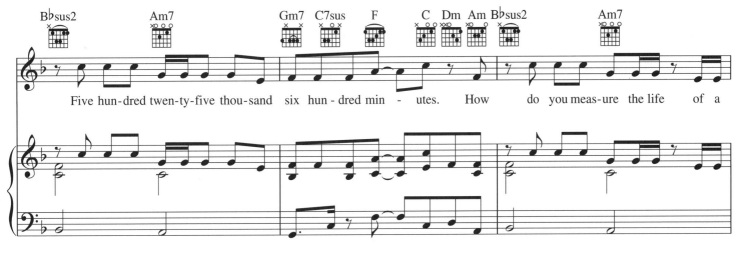

Five hun-dred twen-ty-five thou-sand six hun-dred min - utes. How do you meas-ure the life of a

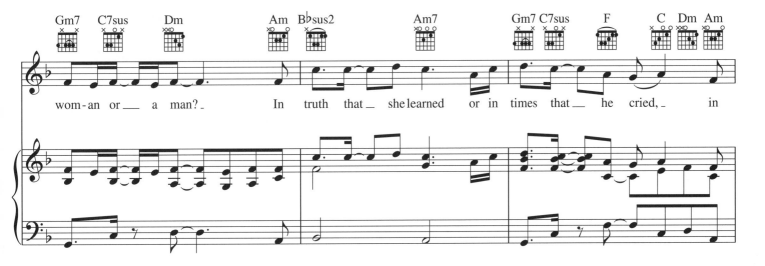

wom-an or ___ a man? ___ In truth that ___ she learned or in times that ___ he cried, __ in

bridg-es ___ he burned or the way that she died. _____ It's time now to sing out, though the

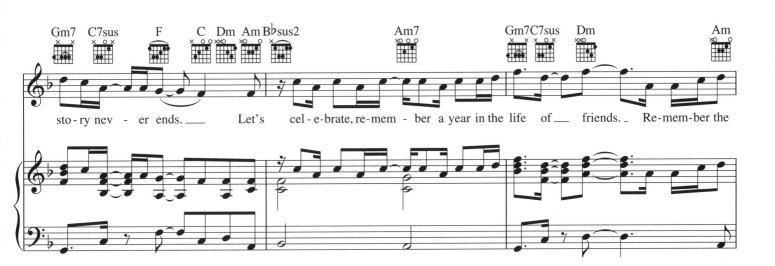

sto-ry nev - er ends. ___ Let's cel-e-brate, re-mem - ber a year in the life of ___ friends. _ Re-mem-ber the

SHE'S GOT A WAY
from MOVIN' OUT

Words and Music by
BILLY JOEL

Slow and steady

She's got a way ___ a - bout ___
She's got a smile ___ that heals ___

___ her.   I don't know ___ what it is, ___   but I
___ me.   I don't know ___ why it is, ___   but I

know   that I ___   can't   live   with - out ___   her.   She's   got   a   way ___   of
have   to   laugh ___   when   she   re - veals ___   me.   She's   got   a   way ___   of

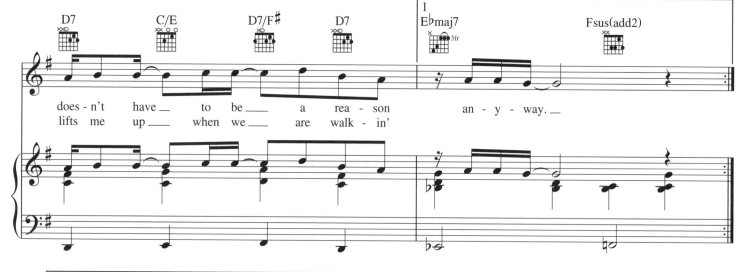

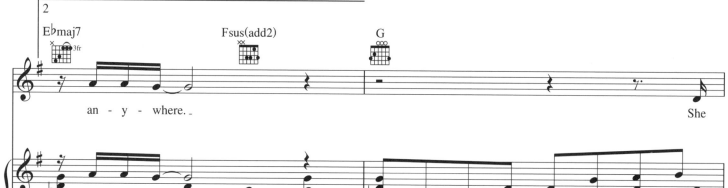

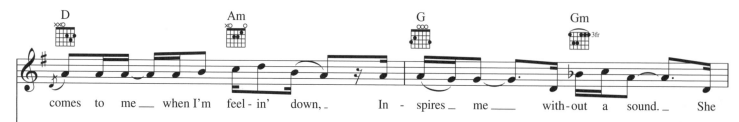

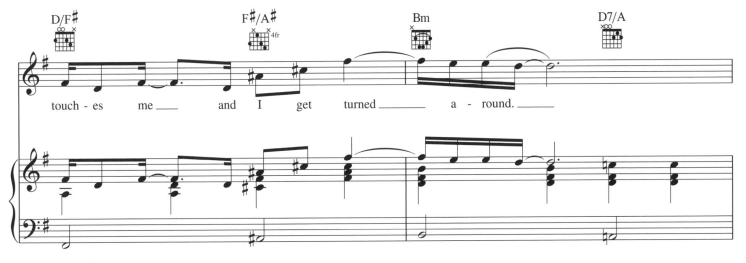

touch - es me ___ and I get turned ___ a - round. ___

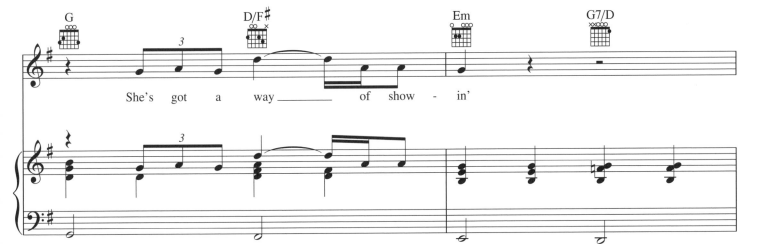

She's got a way ___ of show - in'

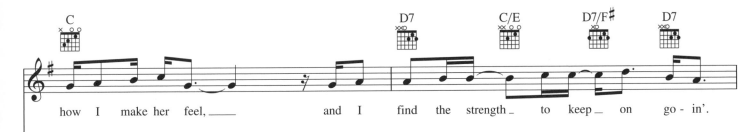

how I make her feel, ___ and I find the strength _ to keep _ on go - in'.

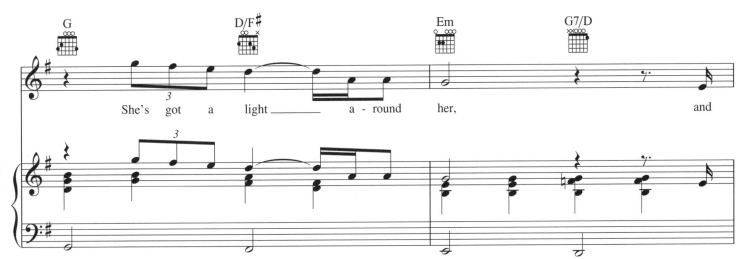

She's got a light ___ a - round her, and

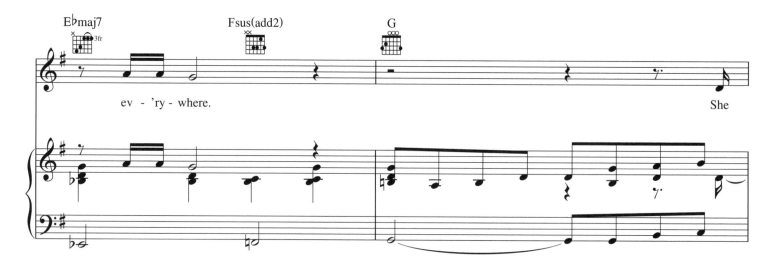

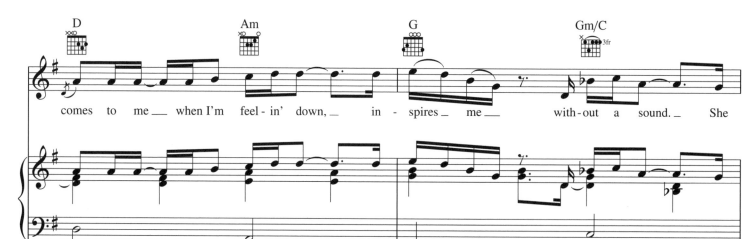

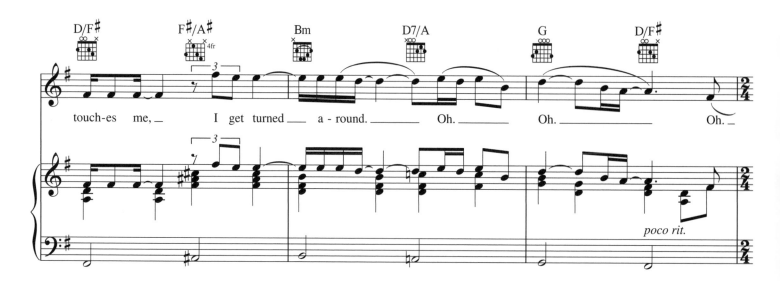

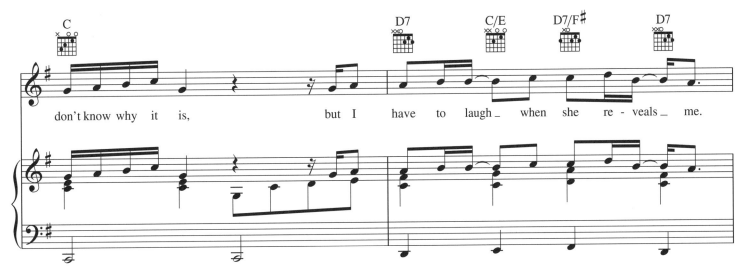

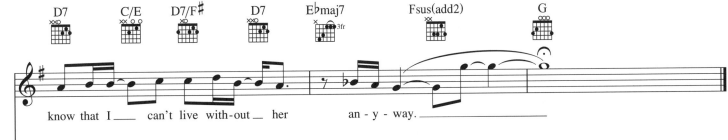

SOMEONE LIKE YOU

from JEKYLL & HYDE

Words by LESLIE BRICUSSE
Music by FRANK WILDHORN

Slowly, with expression

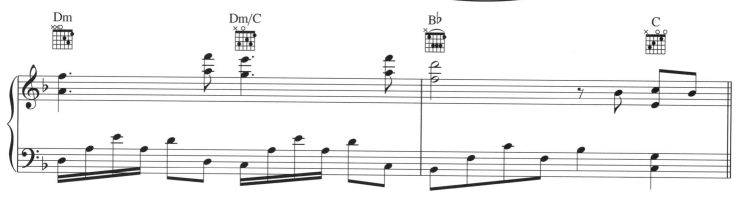

I peered through win-dows, watched life go by. Dreamed of to-mor-row,
It's like you took my dreams, made each one real. You reached in-side of me

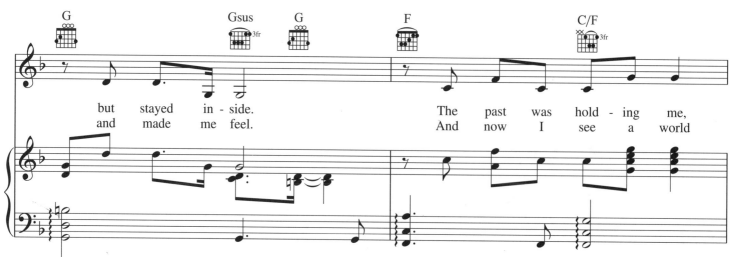

but stayed in-side. The past was hold-ing me,
and made me feel. And now I see a world

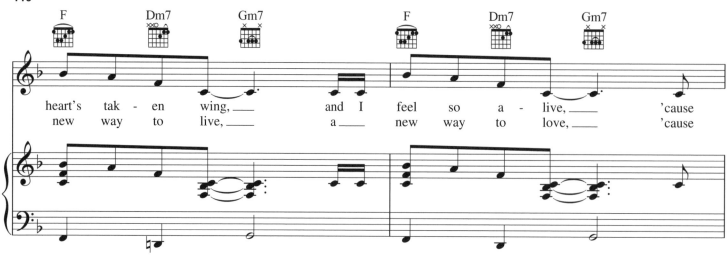

heart's tak - en wing, _____ and I feel so a - live, _____ 'cause
new way to live, _____ a _____ new way to love, _____ 'cause

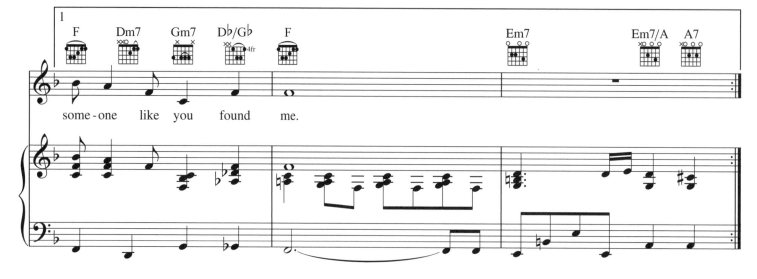

1

some - one like you found me.

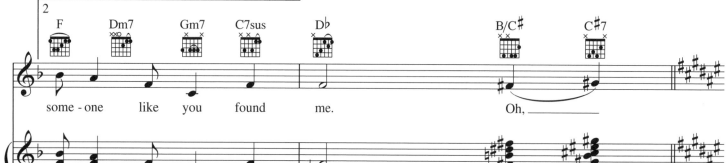

2

some - one like you found me. Oh, _____

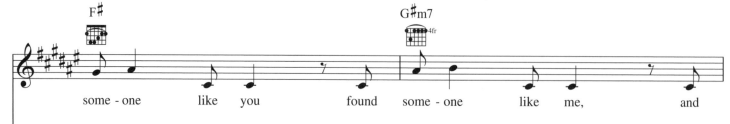

some - one like you found some - one like me, and

sud - den - ly _____ noth - ing will ev - er be the same. My

heart's tak - en wing, _ and I feel so a - live, _____ 'cause

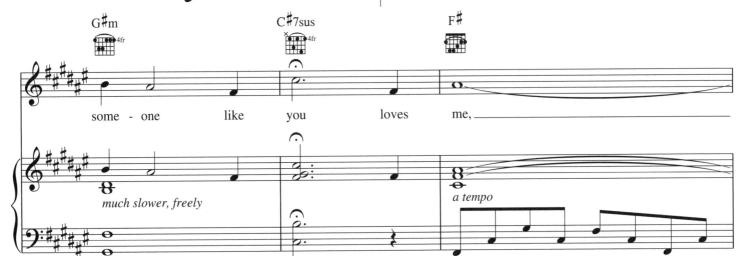

some - one like you loves me, _____

much slower, freely

a tempo

_____ loves _ me. _____

rit.

SUN AND MOON
from MISS SAIGON

Music by CLAUDE-MICHEL SCHÖNBERG
Lyrics by RICHARD MALTBY JR. and ALAIN BOUBLIL
Adapted from original French Lyrics by ALAIN BOUBLIL

You are ___ sun - light ___ and I moon, ___

joined by ___ the gods of for - tune, ___ mid - night ___ and

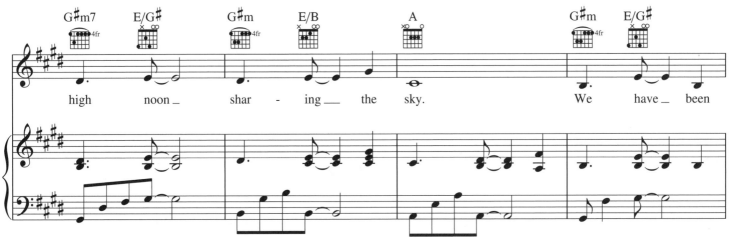

high noon _ shar - ing _ the sky. We have _ been

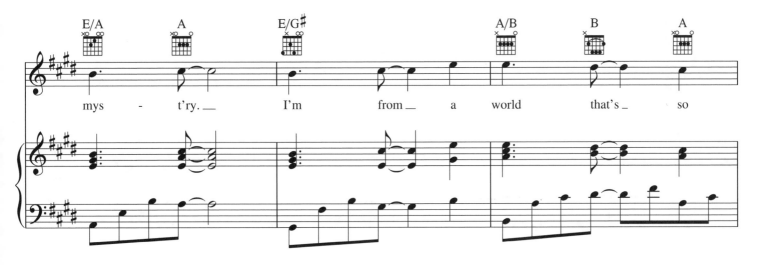

blessed, you _ and I. CHRIS: You are _ here like _ a

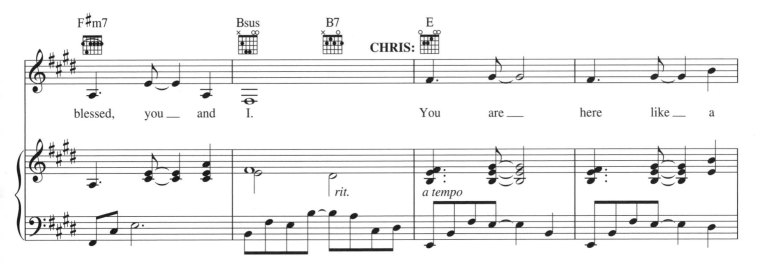

mys - t'ry. _ I'm from _ a world that's _ so

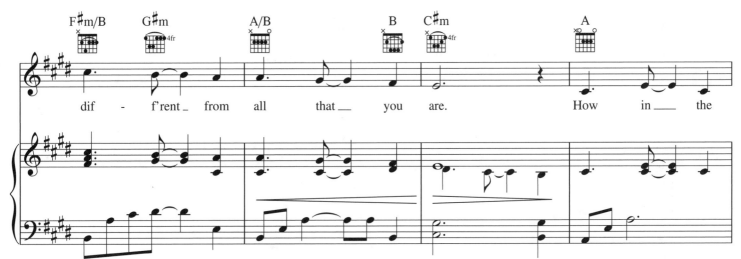

dif - f'rent _ from all that _ you are. How in _ the

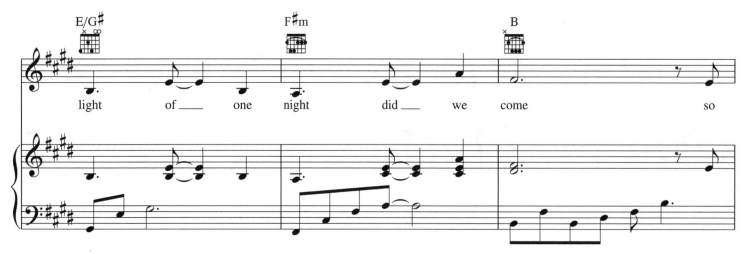

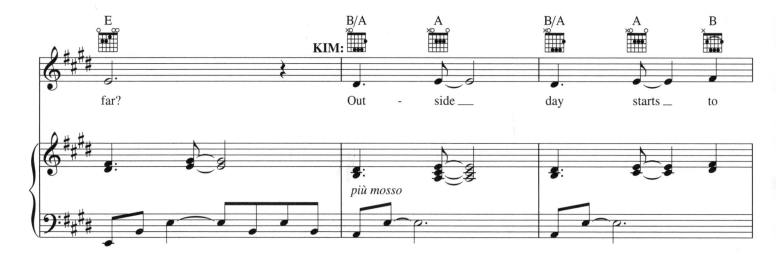

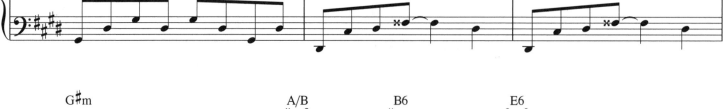

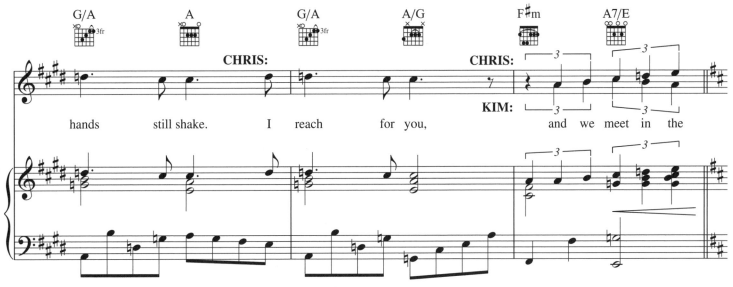

hands still shake. I reach for you, and we meet in the

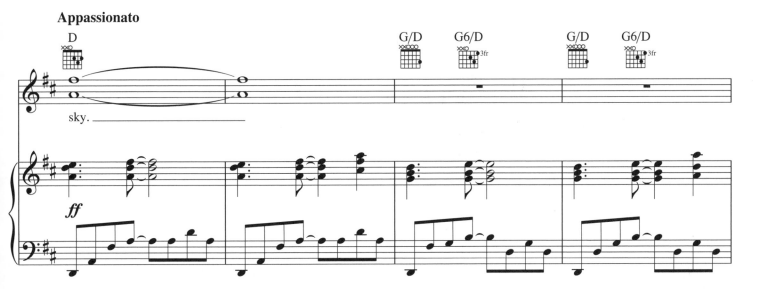

Appassionato

sky. _____

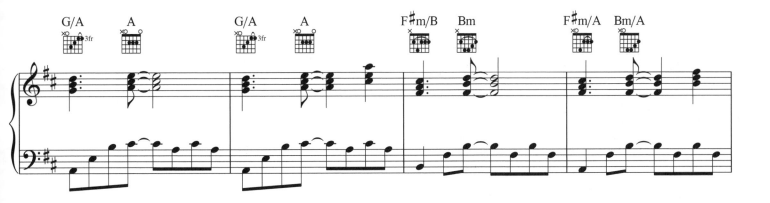

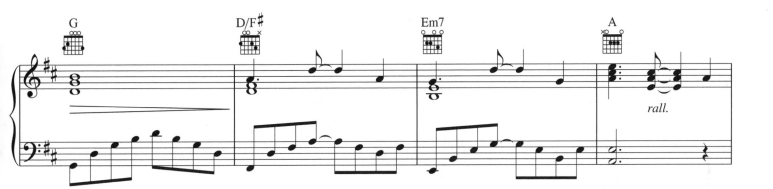

Tranquillo

You are ___ sun - light ___ and I ___ moon, ___

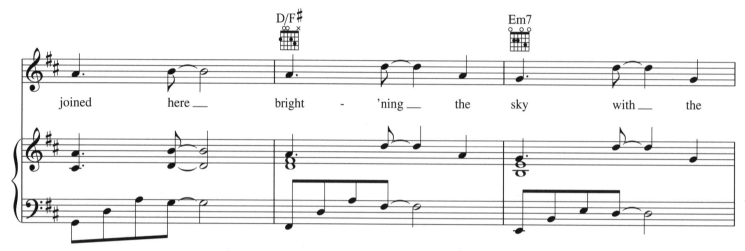

joined here ___ bright - 'ning ___ the sky with ___ the

flame of love. Made of ___

sun - light ___ moon - light.

'TIL HIM
from THE PRODUCERS

Music and Lyrics by
MEL BROOKS

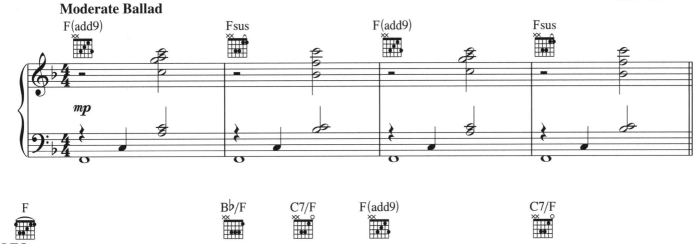

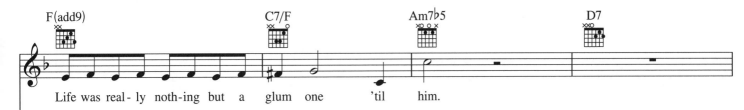

No one ev-er made me feel like some-one 'til him.

Life was real-ly noth-ing but a glum one 'til him.

My ex-ist-ence bor-dered on the trag-ic, al-ways tim-id, nev-er took a

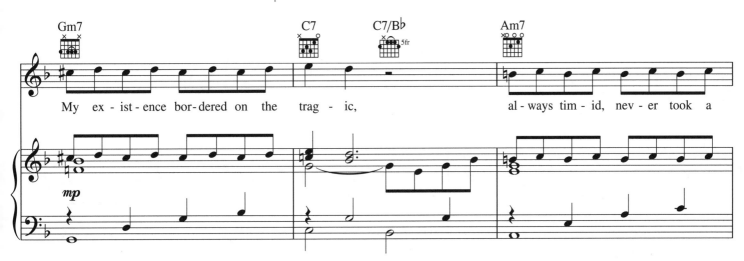

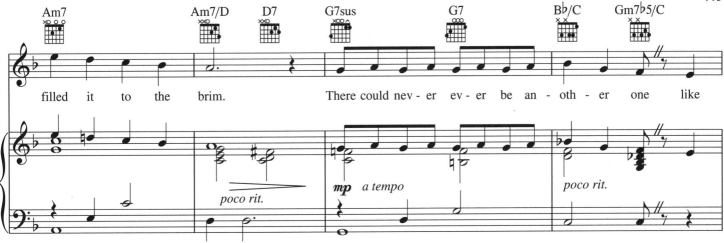

filled it to the brim. There could nev - er ev - er be an - oth - er one like

him.

MAX: No one ev - er ev - er real - ly knew me 'til

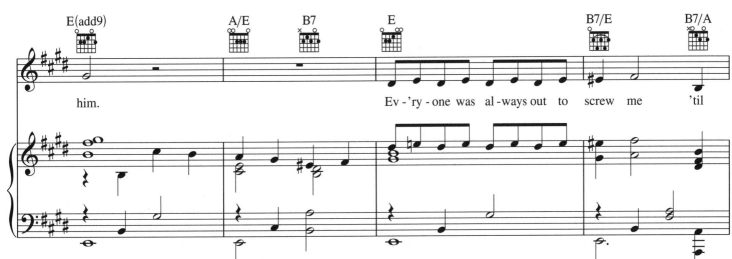

him. Ev - 'ry - one was al - ways out to screw me 'til

Nev- er had a pal to share my trou- bles 'til

him. He filled up my emp- ty life,

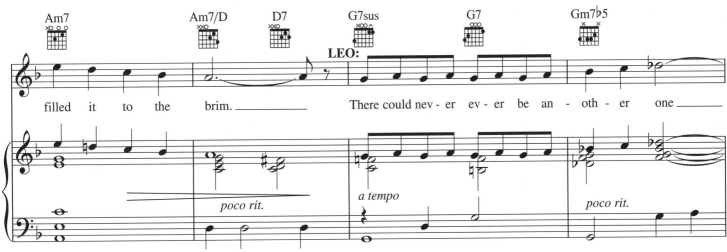

filled it to the brim. There could nev- er ev- er be an- oth- er one

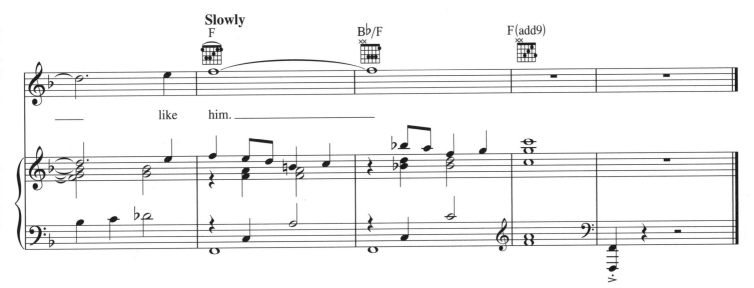

like him.

THAT FACE
from THE PRODUCERS

Music and Lyrics by
MEL BROOKS

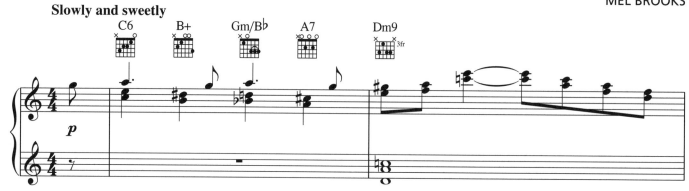

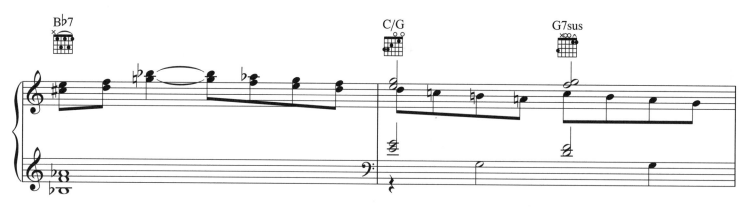

The urge to merge can rob us of our sens - es. The

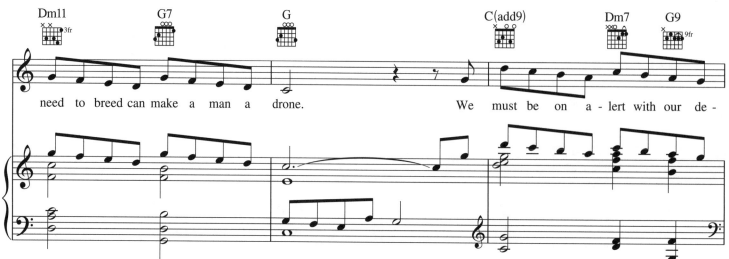

need to breed can make a man a drone. We must be on a - lert with our de -

fens - es   for ev - 'ry skirt will test tes - tos - ter - one.   So

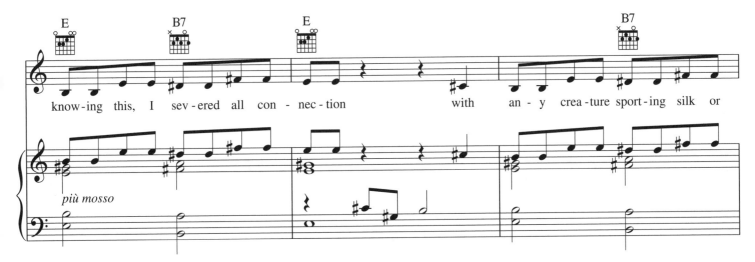

know - ing this, I sev - ered all con - nec - tion   with an - y crea - ture sport - ing silk or

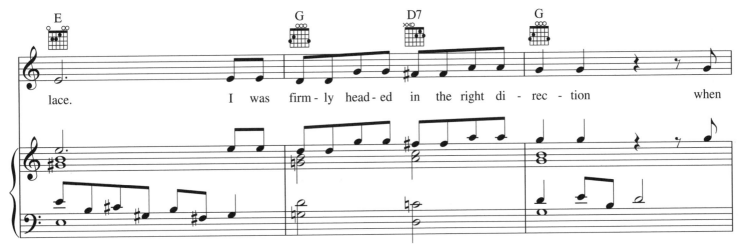

lace.   I was firm - ly head - ed in the right di - rec - tion   when

sud - den - ly I stum - bled on that face.   That

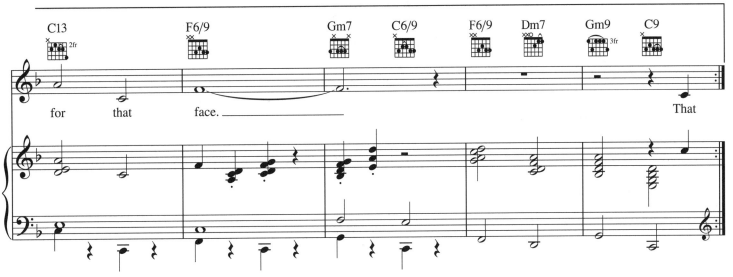

for that face. _____ That

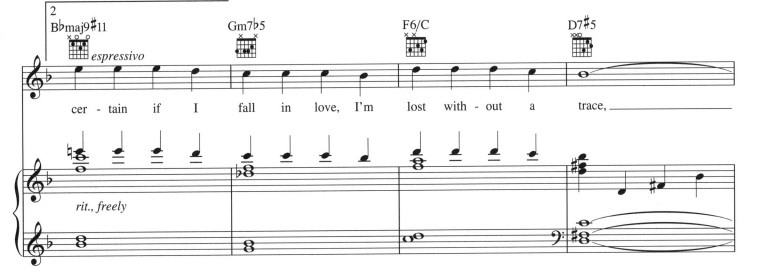

cer - tain if I fall in love, I'm lost with - out a trace, _____

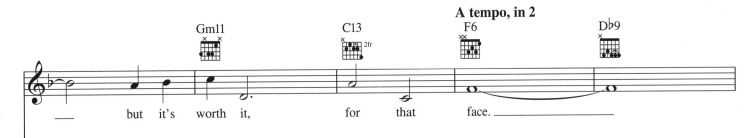

A tempo, in 2

___ but it's worth it, for that face. _____

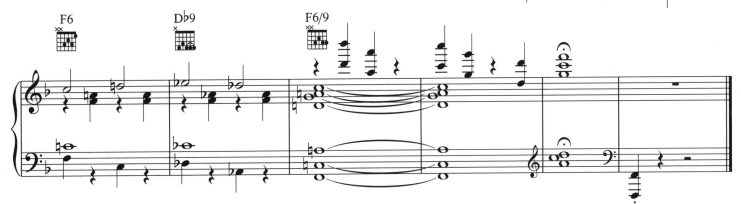

THINK OF ME

from THE PHANTOM OF THE OPERA

Music by ANDREW LLOYD WEBBER
Lyrics by CHARLES HART
Additional Lyrics by RICHARD STILGOE

When you find _____ that once a - gain you long _____ to take your heart back and be

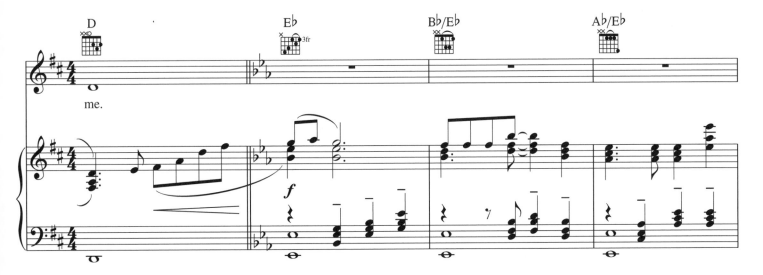

free, if you ev-er find a mo - ment, spare a thought for

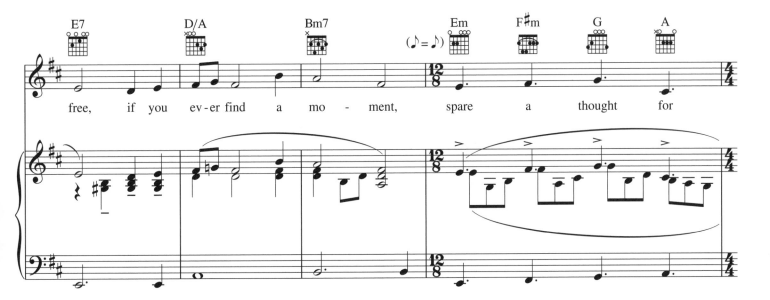

me.

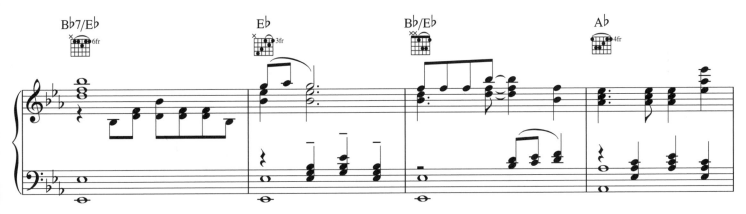

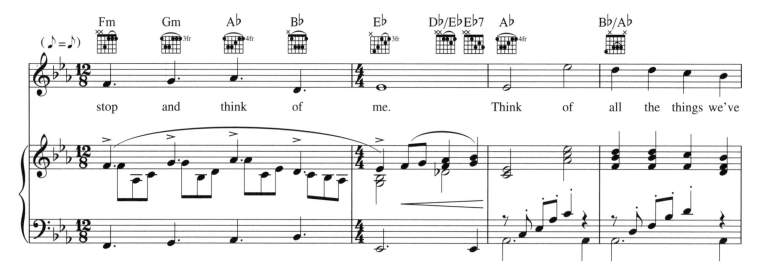

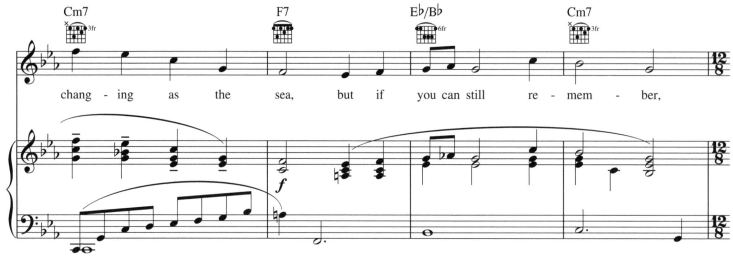

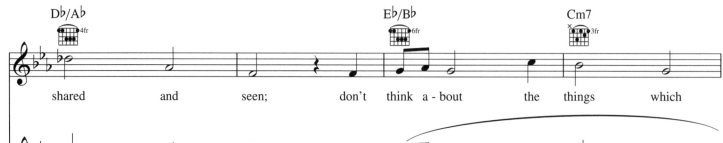

might have been. Think of me, think of me wak - ing

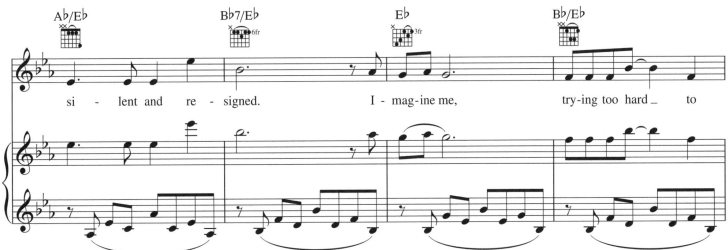

si - lent and re - signed. I - mag-ine me, try-ing too hard _ to

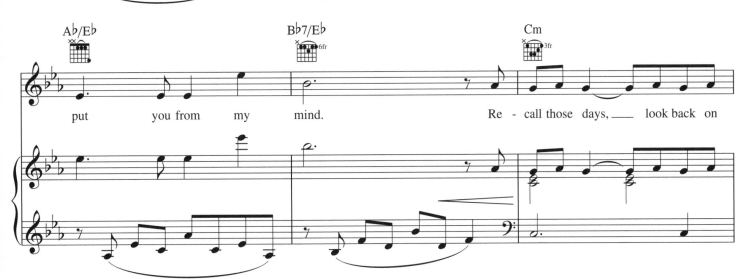

put you from my mind. Re - call those days, ___ look back on

all those times, ___ think of the things we'll nev - er do. There will nev - er be a

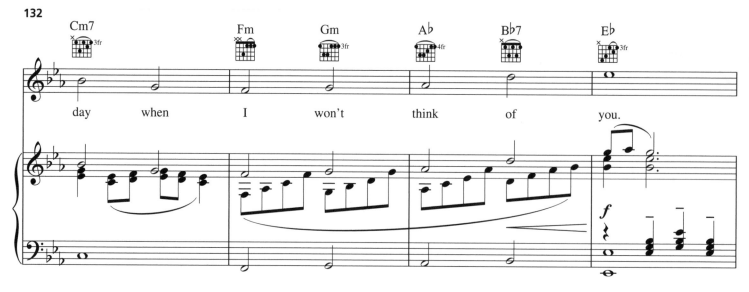

day when I won't think of you.

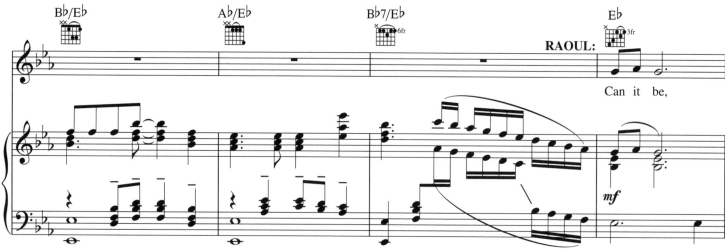

RAOUL:

Can it be,

can it be Chris - tine? What a change, — you're real-ly

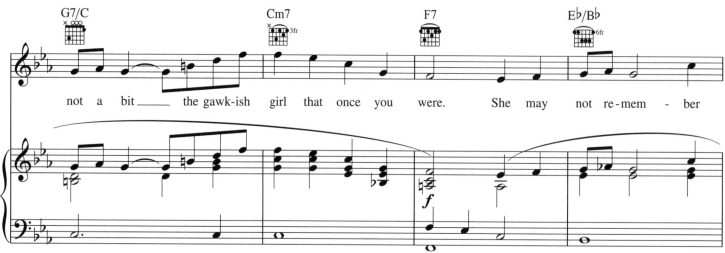

not a bit — the gawk-ish girl that once you were. She may not re-mem - ber

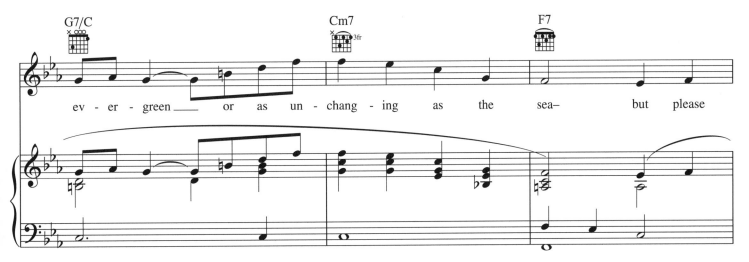

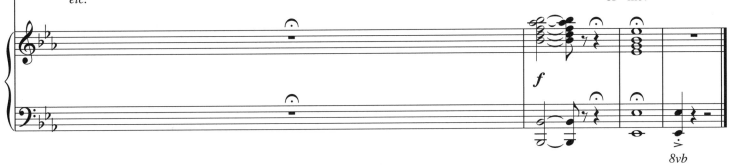

TIMELESS TO ME

from HAIRSPRAY

Music by MARC SHAIMAN
Lyrics by MARC SHAIMAN and SCOTT WITTMAN

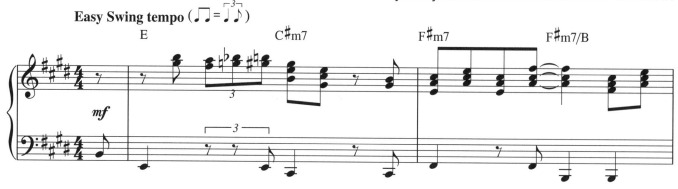

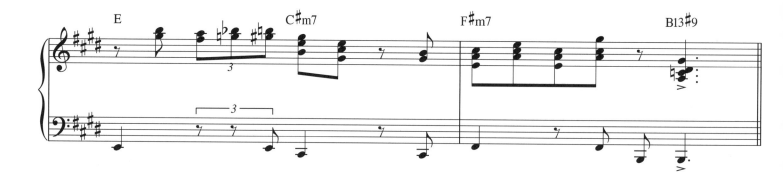

WILBUR:
Styles keep a - chang - in'. The world's re - ar - rang - in', but

Ed - na, you're time - less to me. ____

Hem - lines are short - er. A beer costs a quar - ter, but

time can - not take what comes free. _____

You're like a stink - y old cheese, babe, just get - tin' ri - per with age. _

_ You're like a fa - tal dis - ease, babe, but

there's no cure, so let this fe - ver rage. Some folks can't stand it, say

time is a ban - dit, but I take the op - po - site view. __

__ 'Cause when I need a lift, time __ brings a gift: an -

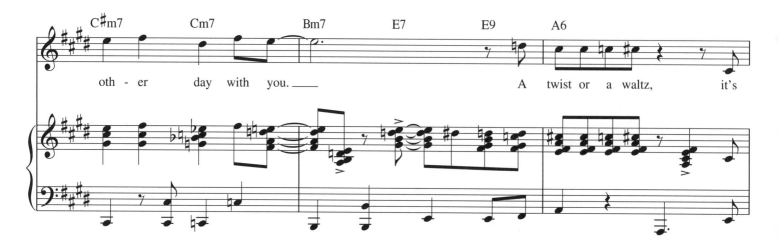

oth - er day with you. __ A twist or a waltz, it's

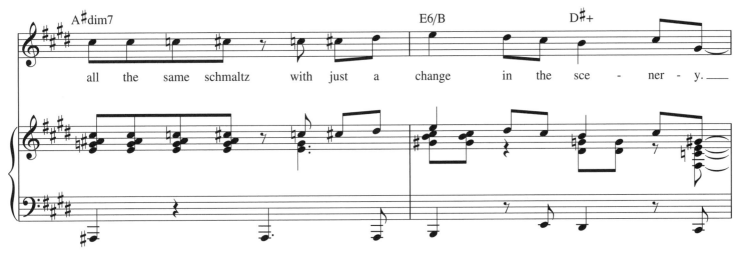

138

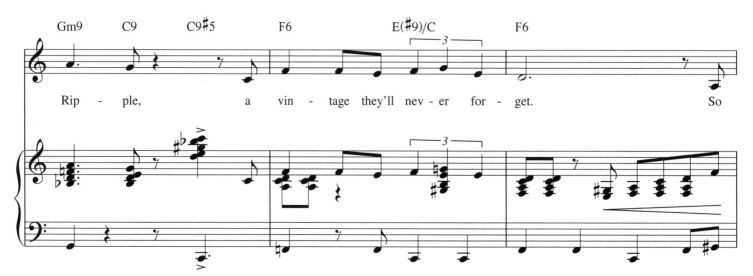

pour me a teen-y ween-y tri-ple ___ and we can toast ___ the fact we

ain't dead yet! I can't stop eat-ing. Your hair - line's re - ced-ing.

Soon there'll be noth - ing at all. _____ So,

you'll wear a wig while I roast a pig. Hey! Pass that Ge - ri - tol! ___

Glenn Mil - ler had class. That Chub - by Check - er's a gas, but they

all pass e - ven - tu - al - ly. _____ You'll nev - er be pas - sé. Hip-hoo-ray!

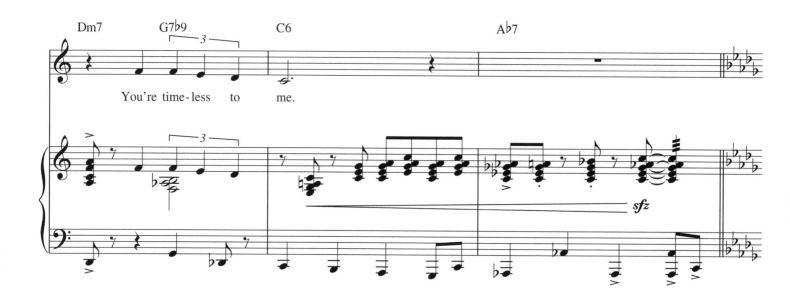

You're time-less to me.

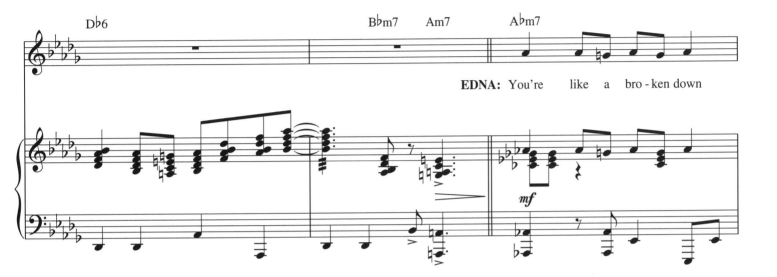

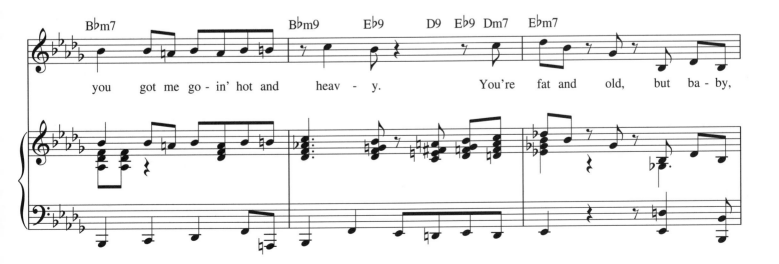

bor - ing you ain't!   **BOTH:** Some folks don't get it, but

we nev - er fret it 'cause we know that time is our friend.

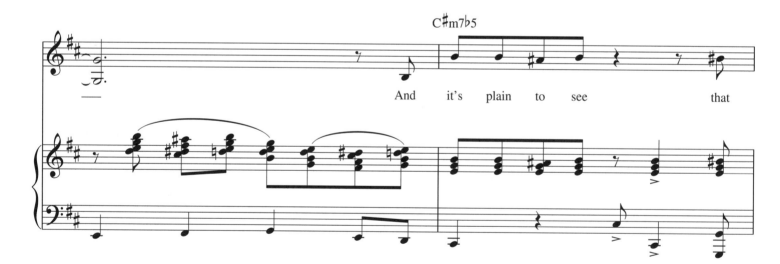

And it's plain to see that

you're stuck with me un - til the bit - ter end.

UNEXPECTED SONG
from SONG & DANCE

Music by ANDREW LLOYD WEBBER
Lyrics by DON BLACK

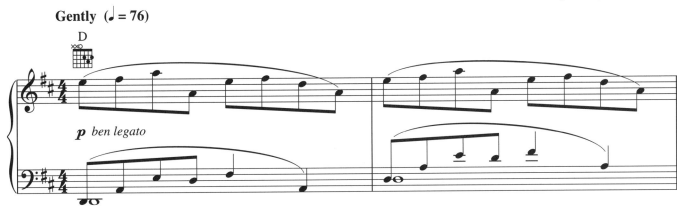

I have nev-er felt like this, for once I'm lost for words, your smile has real-ly
I don't know what's go-ing on, can't work it out at all, what-ev-er made you

thrown me. This is not like me at all, I nev-er thought I'd
choose me? I just can't be-lieve my eyes, you look at me as

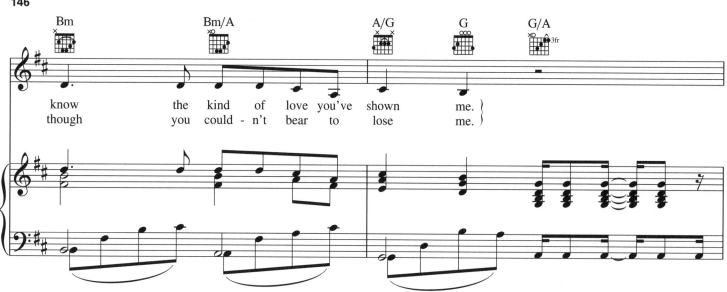

know the kind of love you've shown me.
though you could-n't bear to lose me.

Now, no mat-ter where I am, no mat-ter what I do, I see your face ap-

pear-ing like an un-ex-pect-ed song, an un-ex-pect-ed

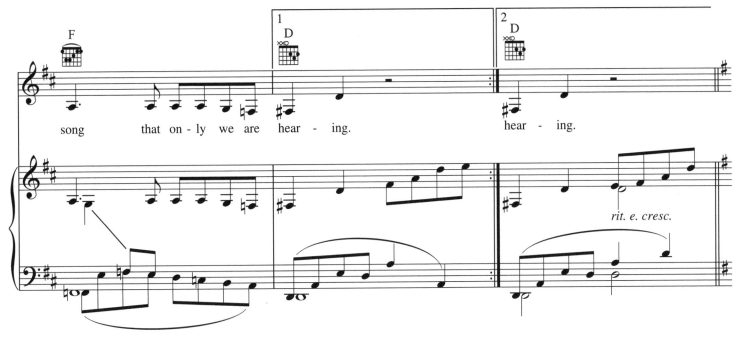

song　that　on - ly　we　are　hear - ing.　　　　hear - ing.

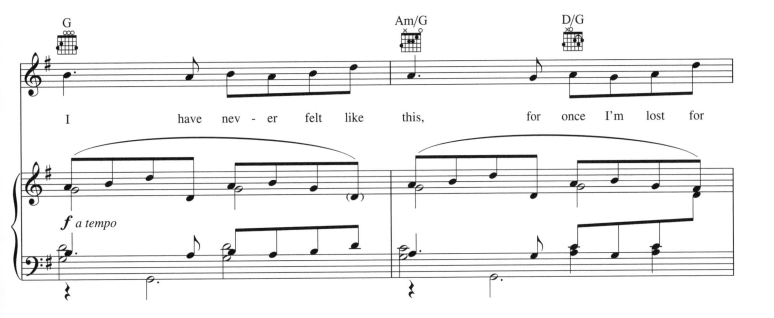

I　have　nev - er　felt　like　this,　　for once I'm lost for

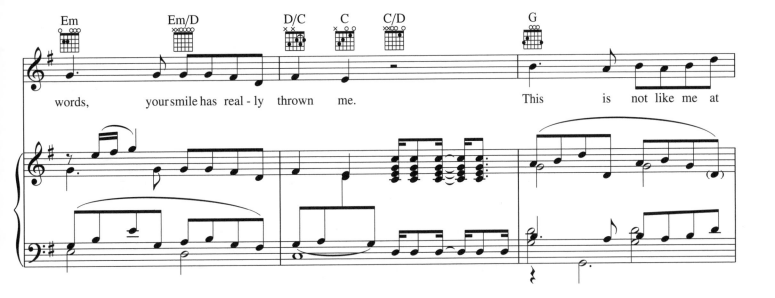

words,　your smile has real - ly　thrown　me.　　This　is　not like me at

all, I nev-er thought I'd know the kind of love you've shown me.

Now, no mat-ter where I am, no mat-ter what I do, I see your face ap-

pear - ing like an un - ex - pect - ed song, an un - ex - pect - ed

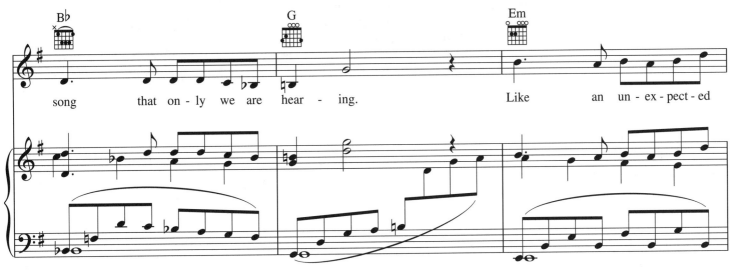

song that on-ly we are hear - ing. Like an un-ex-pect-ed

song, an un-ex-pect-ed song that on-ly we are hear - ing.

TOO MUCH IN LOVE TO CARE
from SUNSET BOULEVARD

Music by ANDREW LLOYD WEBBER
Lyrics by DON BLACK and CHRISTOPHER HAMPTON

When I was a kid __ I played in this street, __ I al - ways loved il -

lu - sion. I thought make be - lieve __ was tru - er than life, __ but now it's all con -

fu - sion. Please can you tell me what's happen - ing? I just don't know an - y -

more. If this is real, how should I feel? What should I look for?

JOE: If you were smart, you would keep on walk-ing

out of my life, as fast as you can. I'm not the one

you should pin your hopes on, you're fall-ing for the

knew where I was, __ I'd giv-en up hope, __ made friends with dis-il -

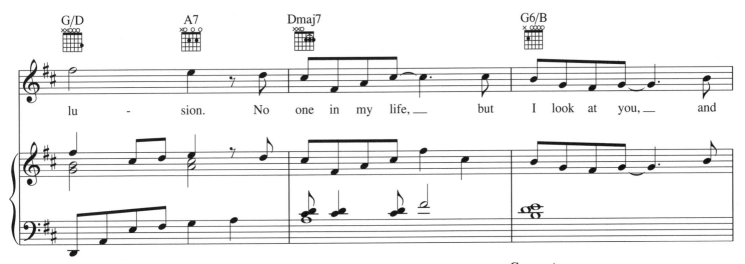

lu - sion. No one in my life, __ but I look at you, __ and

now it's all con - fu - sion. Please can you tell me what's

happen - ing? I just don't know an - y - more.

WHEN I FIRST SAW YOU
from DREAMGIRLS

Music by HENRY KRIEGER
Lyric by TOM EYEN

Moderately slow and free

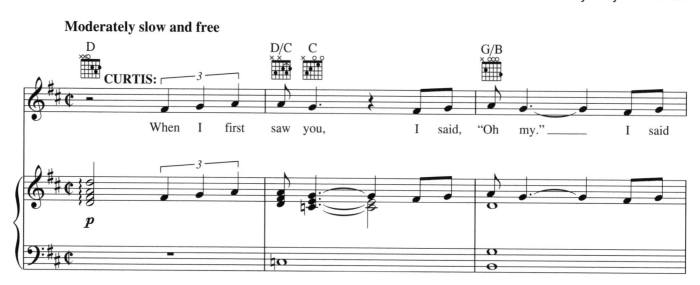

When I first saw you, I said, "Oh my." _____ I said

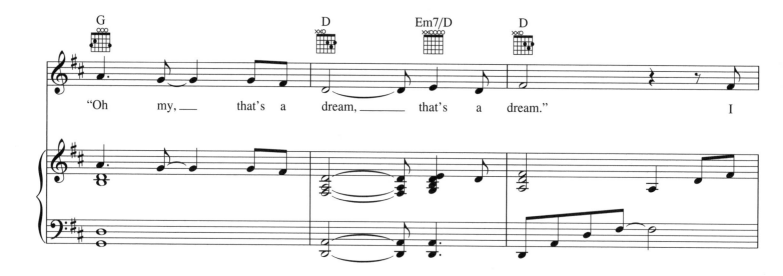

"Oh my, _____ that's a dream, _____ that's a dream." I

need-ed a dream _____ when it all seemed _ to go bad. Then I

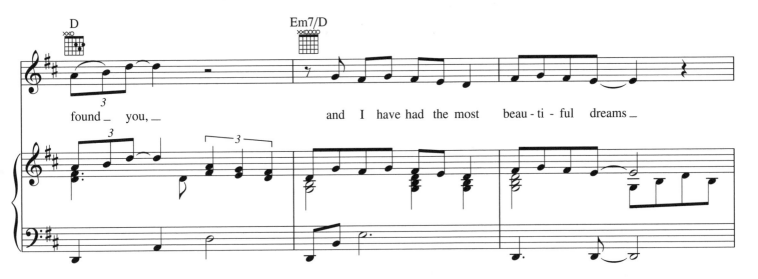

found _ you, _ and I have had the most beau-ti-ful dreams _

an-y man ev-er had. _ When I first saw you, I said,

"Oh my, _____ oh my, _ that's my dream, _____ that's my

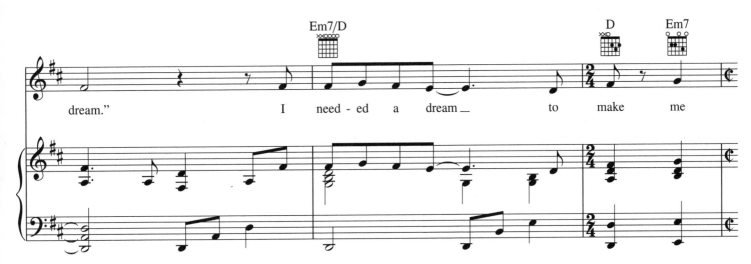

dream." I need-ed a dream _ to make me

strong.

You were the on - ly rea -

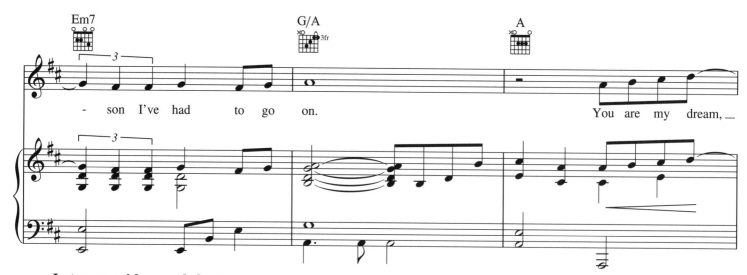

- son I've had to go on.

You are my dream, __

In tempo, with a gentle beat

__ all the things __ I nev - er knew. __

You are my dream. __

Who could be - lieve __ they could ev - er come true? And

who could be-lieve __ the world __ would be-lieve in my dreams, __ too? __

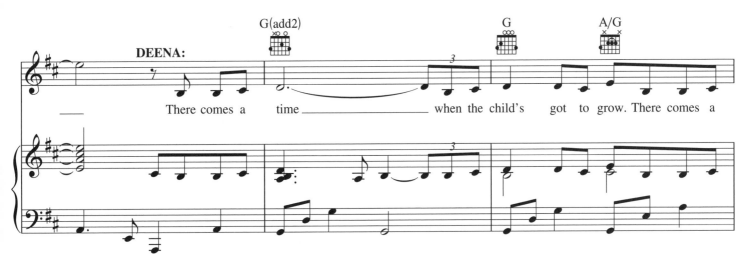

DEENA:

There comes a time ___ when the child's got to grow. There comes a

time when the wom-an's got to go. Ma-ma said I am spe-cial. She

said I've got to prove I am just as good. I'm e-ven bet-ter than. That's

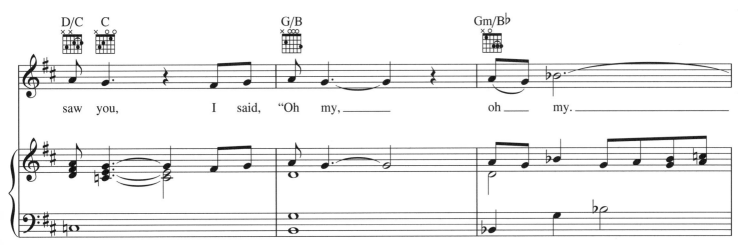

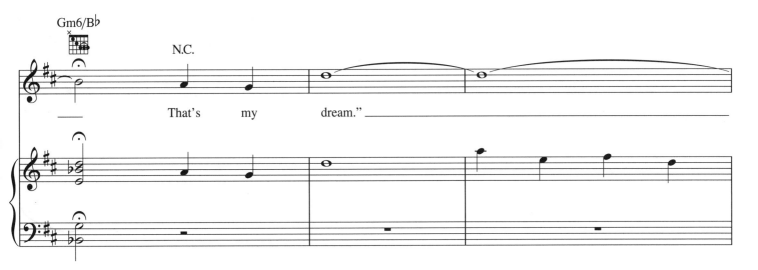

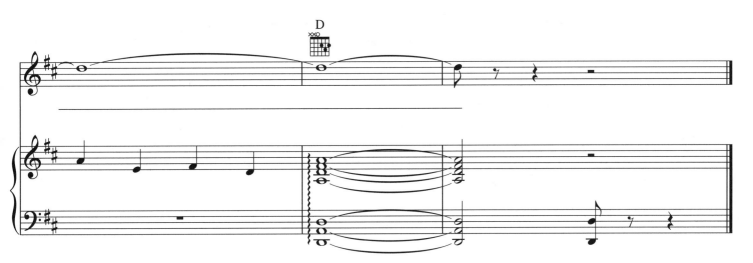

WITHOUT LOVE
from HAIRSPRAY

Music by MARC SHAIMAN
Lyrics by MARC SHAIMAN and SCOTT WITTMAN

Once I was a self-ish fool who nev-er un-der-stood. I

nev-er looked in-side my-self, though on the out-side, I looked good!

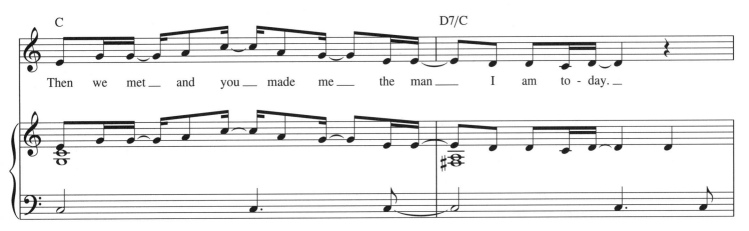

Then we met and you made me the man I am to-day.

Tra - cy, I'm in love with you no mat - ter what you weigh! 'Cause with-out

love, life is like the sea - sons with no sum - mer. With-out

love, life is rock 'n' roll with-out a drum - mer. Tra - cy,

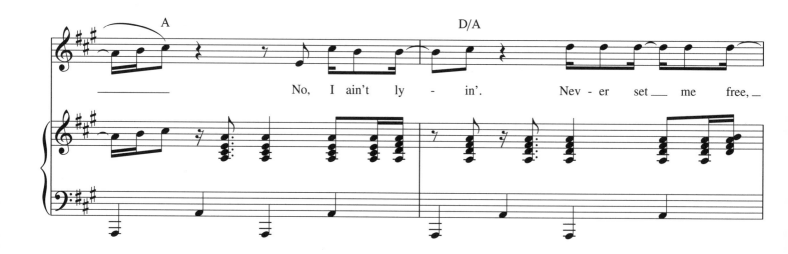

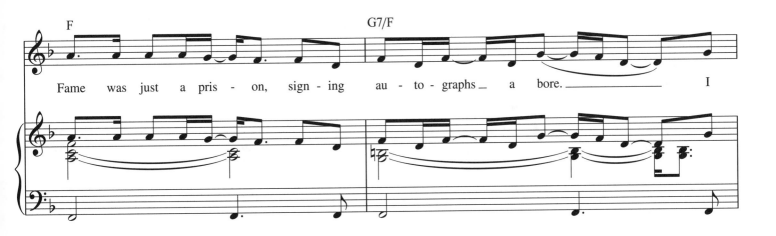

I'm yours for-ev-er. Throw a-way the

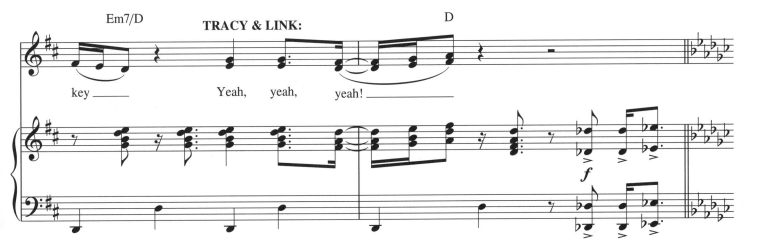

key ___ Yeah, yeah, yeah! ___

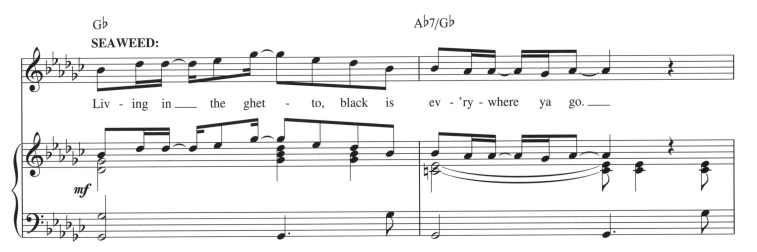

SEAWEED:
Liv-ing in ___ the ghet-to, black is ev-'ry-where ya go. ___

Who'd-'ve thought ___ I'd love ___ a girl ___ with skin as white ___ as win-ter snow? ___

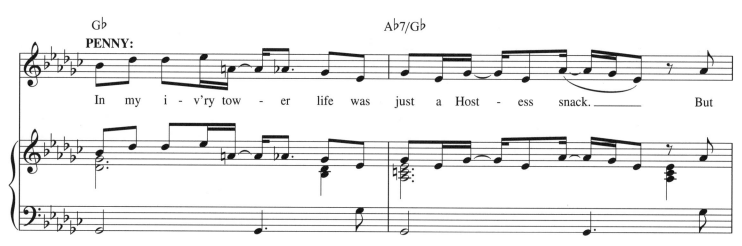

170

I'll be yours for-ev-er 'cause __ I nev-er wan-na be __ with-out

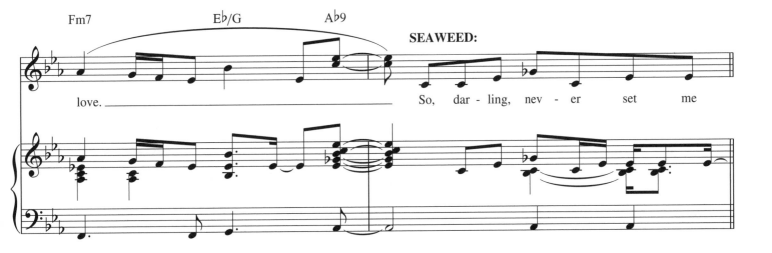

SEAWEED:

love. __ So, dar-ling, nev-er set me

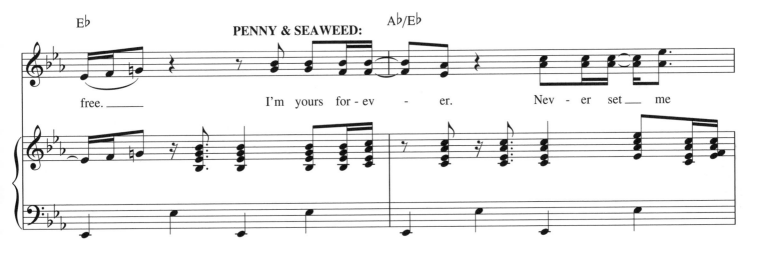

PENNY & SEAWEED:

free. __ I'm yours for-ev-er. Nev-er set __ me

LINK:

free. __ No, no, no! __ If you're

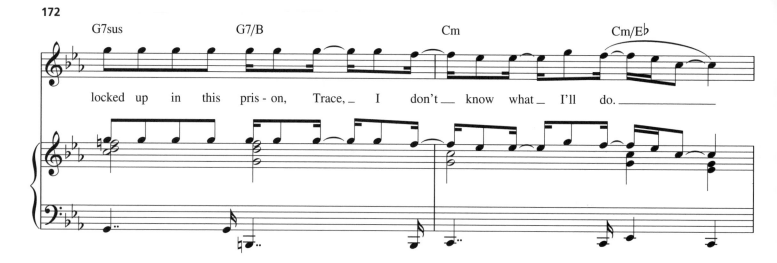

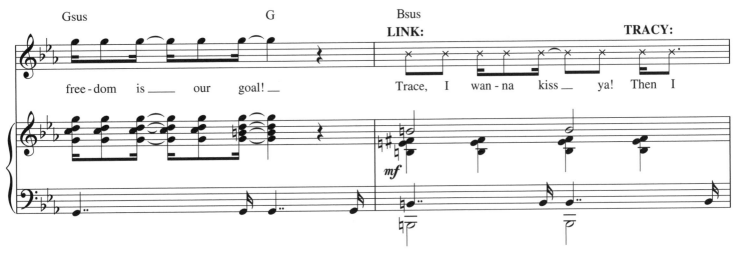

freedom is ___ our goal! ___ Trace, I wan-na kiss ___ ya! Then I

can't wait for pa-role! ___ 'Cause with-out love, life is like ___ a prom ___

___ that won't ___ in-vite ___ us. With-out love, it's like get-ting my ___ big break ___

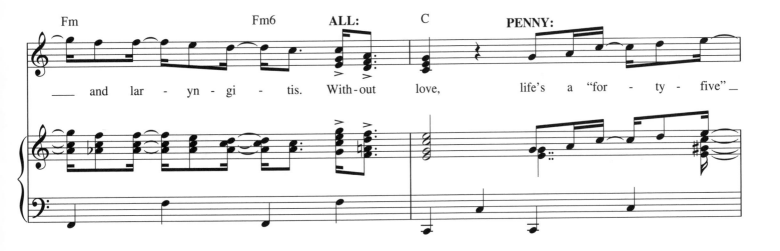

___ and lar-yn-gi-tis. With-out love, life's a "for-ty-five" ___

174

when you __ can't buy __ it. With - out love, life is like __ my

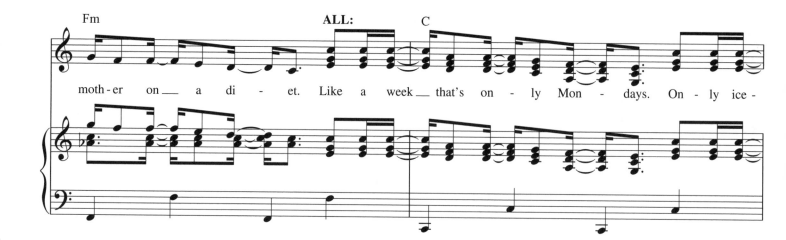

moth - er on __ a di - et. Like a week __ that's on - ly Mon - days. On - ly ice-

- cream, nev - er sun - daes. Like a cir - cle with __ no cen - ter. Like a door __

__ marked "Do Not En - ter!" Dar - ling, I'll be yours for - ev - er 'cause I

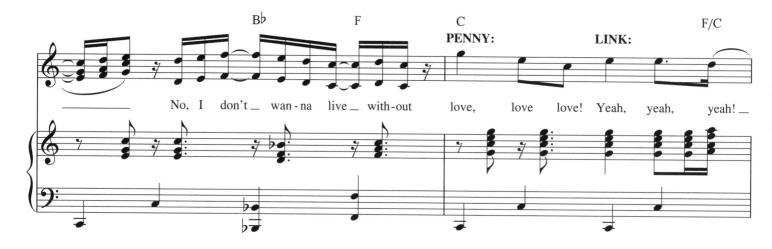

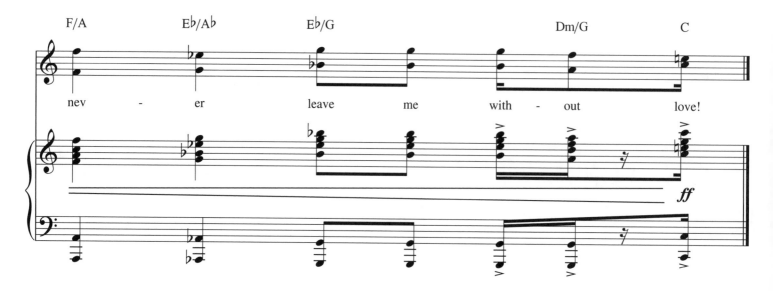

WITHOUT YOU
from RENT

Words and Music by
JONATHAN LARSON

Moderately flowing

With pedal

With - out you, _____ the ground thaws, _____
out you, _____ the breeze warms, _____
out you, _____ the hand gropes, _____

_____ the rain falls, _____ the grass grows. _____
_____ the girl smiles, _____ the cloud moves. _____
_____ the ear hears, _____ the pulse beats. _____

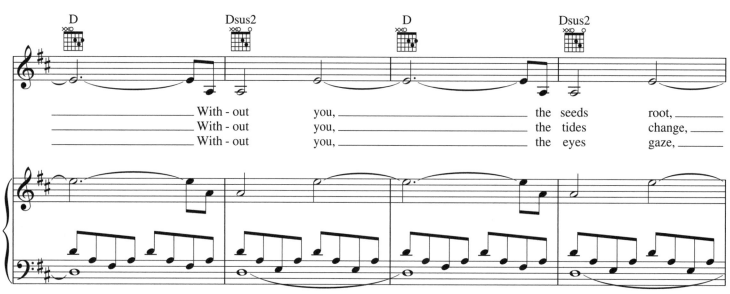

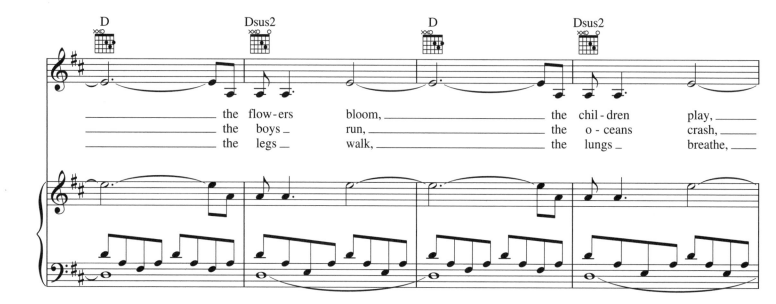

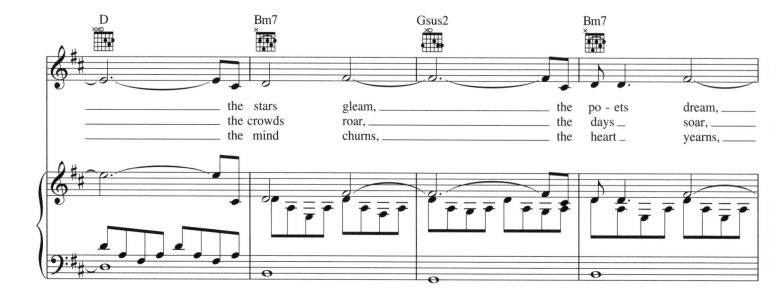

the ea - gles fly _____ with - out _____ you. _____
the ba - bies cry _____ with - out _____ you. _____
the tears _____ dry _____ with - out _____ you.

To Coda

The earth turns, _____ the
The moon glows, _____ the
Life goes on, _____ but

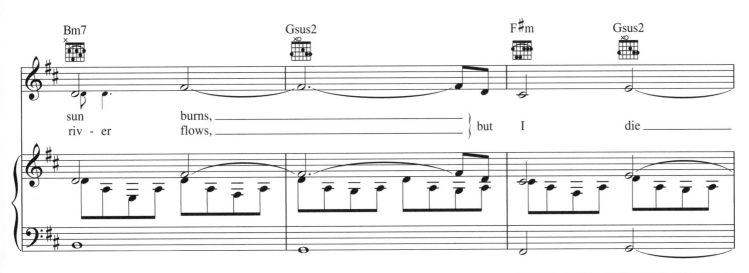

sun burns, _____ but I die _____
riv - er flows, _____

with - out _____ you. _____

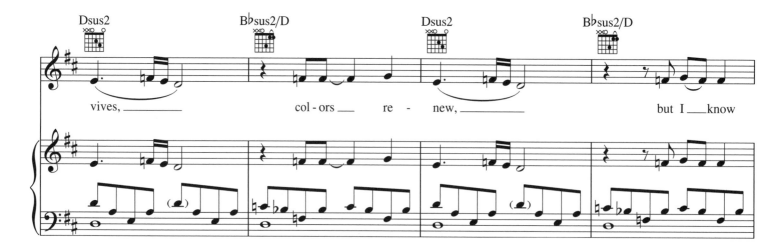

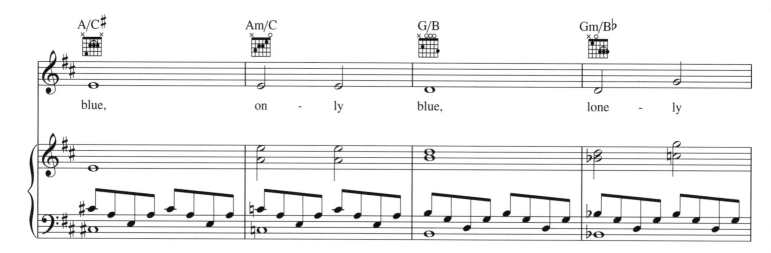

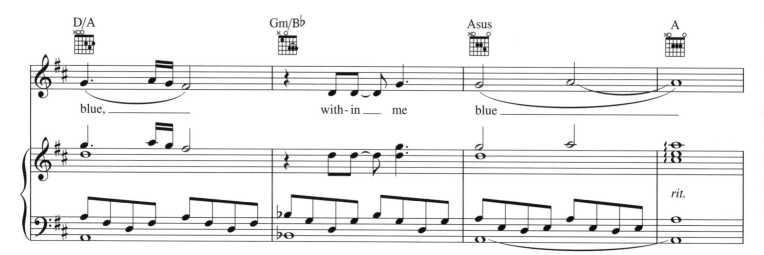

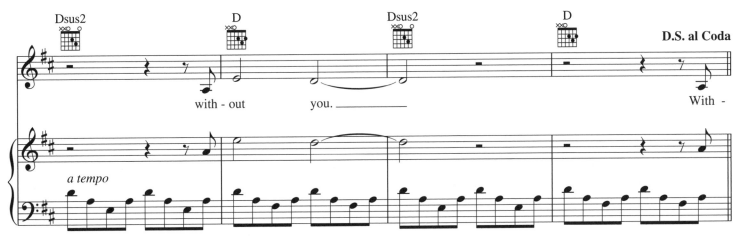

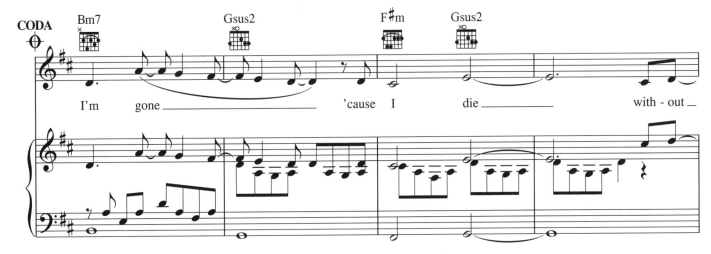
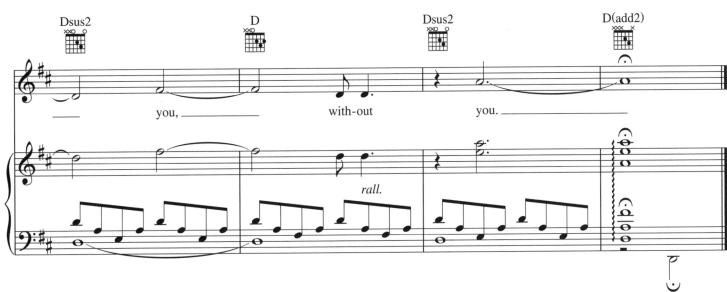

YOU WALK WITH ME

from THE FULL MONTY

Words and Music by
DAVID YAZBEK

Moderately slow, but moving ahead

MALCOLM: Is it the wind ___ o-ver my shoul-der? ___ Is it the wind that I hear gen-tly whis-per-ing,

"Are you a - lone ___ there in the val - ley?" ___

mp

poco rit.

a tempo

*Sing the top line melody in this section for a solo version of the song.

YOU'LL BE IN MY HEART

Disney Presents TARZAN™ The Broadway Musical

Words and Music by
PHIL COLLINS

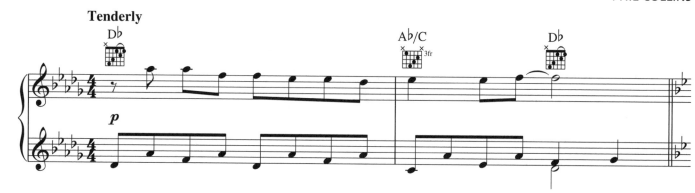

Come stop your cry-ing, it will be al-right. Just take my hand,

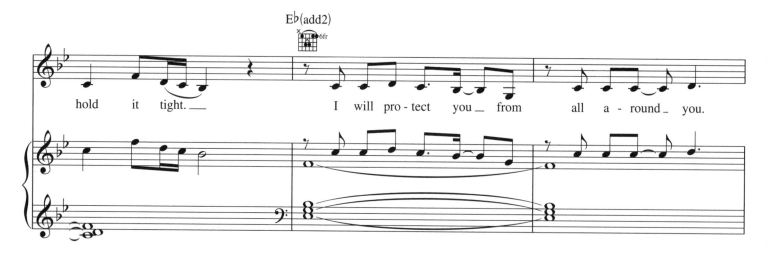

hold it tight. I will pro-tect you from all a-round you.

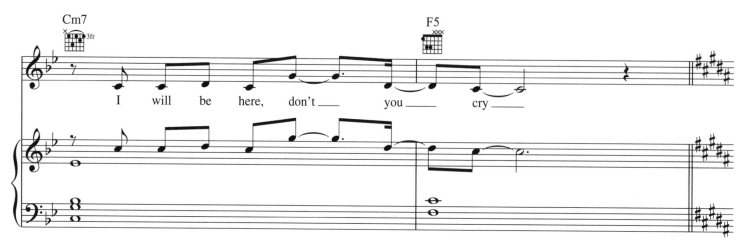

I will be here, don't you cry

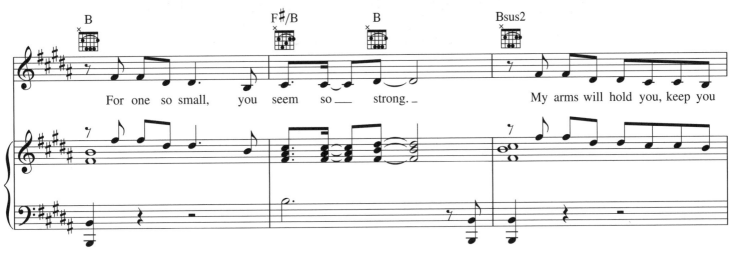

For one so small, you seem so strong. My arms will hold you, keep you

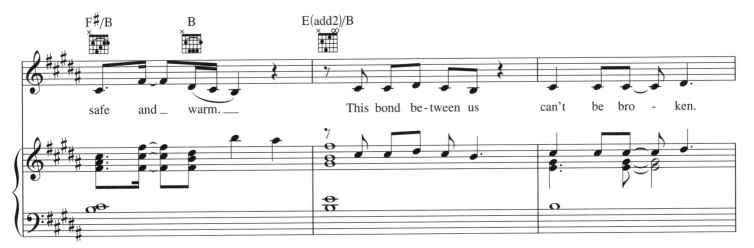

safe and warm. This bond be-tween us can't be bro-ken.

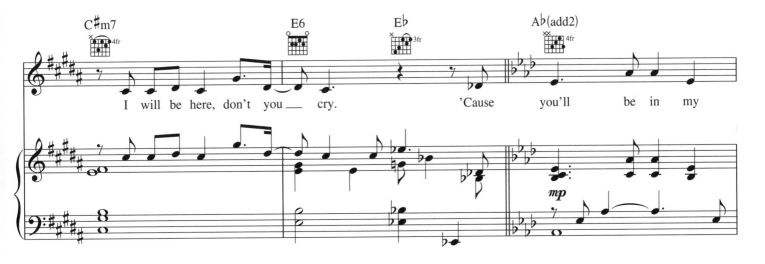

I will be here, don't you cry. 'Cause you'll be in my

heart. Yes, you'll be in my heart from

188

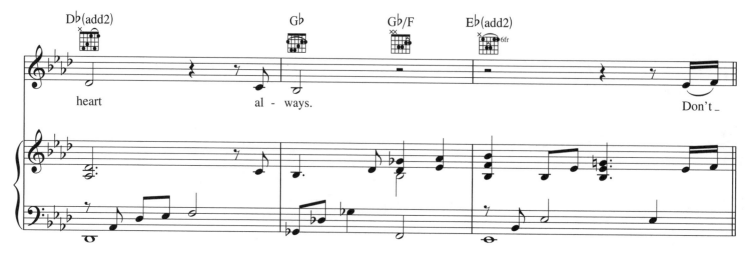

The Most Romantic Music In The World

Arranged for piano, voice, and guitar

The Best Love Songs Ever - 2nd Edition

This revised edition includes 65 romantic favorites: Always • Beautiful in My Eyes • Can You Feel the Love Tonight • Endless Love • Have I Told You Lately • Misty • Something • Through the Years • Truly • When I Fall in Love • and more.

00359198 ....$19.95

The Big Book of Love Songs - 2nd Edition

80 romantic hits in many musical styles: Always on My Mind • Cherish • Fields of Gold • I Honestly Love You • I'll Be There • Isn't It Romantic? • Lady • My Heart Will Go On • Save the Best for Last • Truly • Wonderful Tonight • and more.

00310784 ....$19.95

The Christian Wedding Songbook

37 songs of love and commitment, including: Bonded Together • Cherish the Treasure • Flesh of My Flesh • Go There with You • Household of Faith • How Beautiful • I Will Be Here • Love Will Be Our Home • Make Us One • Parent's Prayer • This Is the Day • This Very Day • and more.

00310681 ....$16.95

The Bride's Guide to Wedding Music

This great guide is a complete resource for planning wedding music. It includes a thorough article on choosing music for a wedding ceremony, and 65 songs in many different styles to satisfy lots of different tastes. The songs are grouped by categories, including preludes, processionals, recessionals, traditional sacred songs, popular songs, country songs, contemporary Christian songs, Broadway numbers, and new age piano music.

00310615 ....$19.95

Broadway Love Songs

50 romantic favorites from shows such as *Phantom of the Opera, Guys and Dolls, Oklahoma!, South Pacific, Fiddler on the Roof* and more. Songs include: All I Ask of You • Bewitched • I've Grown Accustomed to Her Face • Love Changes Everything • So in Love • Sunrise, Sunset • Unexpected Song • We Kiss in a Shadow • and more.

00311558 ....$15.95

Country Love Songs - 4th Edition

This edition features 34 romantic country favorites: Amazed • Breathe • Could I Have This Dance • Forever and Ever, Amen • I Need You • The Keeper of the Stars • Love Can Build a Bridge • One Boy, One Girl • Stand by Me • This Kiss • Through the Years • Valentine • You Needed Me • more.

00311528 ....$14.95

The Definitive Love Collection - 2nd Edition

100 romantic favorites – all in one convenient collection! Includes: All I Ask of You • Can't Help Falling in Love • Endless Love • The Glory of Love • Have I Told You Lately • Heart and Soul • Lady in Red • Love Me Tender • My Romance • So in Love • Somewhere Out There • Unforgettable • Up Where We Belong • When I Fall in Love • and more!

00311681 ....$24.95

I Will Be Here

Over two dozen romantic selections from top contemporary Christian artists such as Susan Ashton, Avalon, Steven Curtis Chapman, Twila Paris, Sonicflood, and others. Songs include: Answered Prayer • Beautiful in My Eyes • Celebrate You • For Always • Give Me Forever (I Do) • Go There with You • How Beautiful • Love Will Be Our Home • and more.

00306472 ....$17.95

Love Songs
Budget Books Series

74 favorite love songs, including: And I Love Her • Cherish • Crazy • Endless Love • Fields of Gold • I Just Called to Say I Love You • I'll Be There • (You Make Me Feel Like) A Natural Woman • Wonderful Tonight • You Are So Beautiful • and more.

00310834 ....$12.95

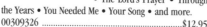

The New Complete Wedding Songbook

41 of the most requested and beloved songs for romance and weddings: Anniversary Song • Ave Maria • Canon in D (Pachelbel) • Could I Have This Dance • Endless Love • I Love You Truly • Just the Way You Are • The Lord's Prayer • Through the Years • You Needed Me • Your Song • and more.

00309326 ....$12.95

New Ultimate Love and Wedding Songbook

This whopping songbook features 90 songs of devotion, including: The Anniversary Waltz • Can't Smile Without You • Could I Have This Dance • Endless Love • For All We Know • Forever and Ever, Amen • The Hawaiian Wedding Song • Here, There and Everywhere • I Only Have Eyes for You • Just the Way You Are • Longer • The Lord's Prayer • Love Me Tender • Misty • Somewhere • Sunrise, Sunset • Through the Years • Trumpet Voluntary • Your Song • and more.

00361445 ....$19.95

Romance - Boleros Favoritos

Features 48 Spanish and Latin American favorites: Aquellos Ojos Verdes • Bésame Mucho • El Reloj • Frenes • Inolvidable • La Vida Es Un Sueño • Perfidia • Siempre En Mi Corazón • Solamente Una Vez • more.

00310383 ....$16.95

Soulful Love Songs

Features 35 favorite romantic ballads, including: All My Life • Baby, Come to Me • Being with You • Endless Love • Hero • I Just Called to Say I Love You • I'll Make Love to You • I'm Still in Love with You • Killing Me Softly with His Song • My Cherie Amour • My Eyes Adored You • Oh Girl • On the Wings of Love • Overjoyed • Tonight, I Celebrate My Love • Vision of Love • You Are the Sunshine of My Life • You've Made Me So Very Happy • and more.

00310922 ....$14.95

Selections from VH1's 100 Greatest Love Songs

Nearly 100 love songs chosen for their emotion. Includes: Always on My Mind • Baby, I Love Your Way • Careless Whisper • Endless Love • How Deep Is Your Love • I Got You Babe • If You Leave Me Now • Love Me Tender • My Heart Will Go On • Unchained Melody • You're Still the One • and dozens more!

00306506 ....$27.95

1004